THE ACTOR'S BOOK
OF
MOVIE
MONOLOGUES

EDITED BY
Marisa Smith and Amy Schewel

D0029022

PENGUIN BOOKS

PENGUIN BOOKS
Published by the Penguin Group
Penguin Books USA Inc.,
375 Hudson Street, New York, New York 10014, U.S.A.
Penguin Books Ltd, 27 Wrights Lane, London W8 5TZ, England
Penguin Books Australia Ltd, Ringwood, Victoria, Australia
Penguin Books Canada Ltd, 10 Alcorn Avenue,
Toronto, Ontario, Canada M4V 3B2
Penguin Books (N.Z.) Ltd, 182–190 Wairau Road, Auckland 10, New Zealand

Penguin Books Ltd, Registered Offices:
Harmondsworth, Middlesex, England

First published in Penguin Books 1986
Published simultaneously in Canada

19   20

LIBRARY OF CONGRESS CATALOGING IN PUBLICATION DATA
The Actor's book of movie monologues.
1. Moving-picture acting.   2. Monologues.   I. Smith,
Marisa.   II. Schewel, Amy.
PN1995.A259   1986   791.43′028   86-8093
ISBN 0 14 00.9475 X

Printed in the United States of America
Set in Caledonia and Gill Sans
Designed by Robert Bull

ACKNOWLEDGMENTS

The editors wish to thank the following: Charles Silver and the staff at the Museum of Modern Art Film Study Center, as well as the staff of the Museum of Modern Art Library; the staff of the Theater Collection of the New York Public Library at Lincoln Center; the staff of the Script Collection at The Elmer Holmes Bobst Library, New York University; Herbert Nussbaum at MGM/UA; Pam North at Twentieth Century-Fox; Joan Salzman at Columbia Pictures; Jeremy Williams at Warner Brothers, Inc.; Nancy Cushing-Jones and Laurie Rodich at MCA-Universal; Edith Tolkin and Steven Kotlowitz at Paramount; Elizabeth Pond at Zoetrope Studios; Jody Hotchkiss; John Sayles; Jean Passanante; Kate Green; Douglas Green; Mary Cleere Haran; Maggie Renzi; Peggy Rajski; Jack Shannon; Ellis Levine; Jeffrey Lane; Eric Lane; David Rivell; John Heffernan; Cornelia Wallin; Chris Robinson; Bill Treusch; Gail Obenrader; Richard Babcock; David Strathairn; Logan Goodman; Marc Routh; Kate Clark; Russell Schwartz; John Rothman; Jill Silverman; Winnie Holzman; Marjorie Gordon; William and Madlyn Smith; Robert and Paul Barsa at Uptown Video, Hoboken, New Jersey; Elizabeth Arnac; Gloria Stone; the I. Stanley Kriegel Office; Alicia Stone; Robert Kravitz; David Babcock; Diana Finch of the Ellen Levine Agency; J. B. White; and Eric Kraus.

And finally, we thank Smith & Kraus, Inc., where the book was conceived and where we were provided whatever help needed to complete the book.

CONTENTS

PREFACE

The search for a "better" monologue is a virtually unending quest for every acting student or professional actor. The monologue is both the universally accepted audition piece and an essential tool for developing acting skills in the classroom. Yet until now no one has compiled a book of movie monologues, leaving a great source of material largely inaccessible to the general public. Most of the monologues in this book were drawn from unpublished scripts in libraries, studio archives, and private collections. Where no scripts were available, we transcribed the dialogue directly from the screen.

The essential criterion of a monologue selected for inclusion in this book is that it provide the actor with a complete moment to play. These monologues also represent a broad range of roles and emotions—from the energetic bombast of Gantry in *Elmer Gantry* as he extols the power of divine love to the desperate yet hilarious near breakdown of Alison, the failed actress in *Who Is Harry Kellerman and Why Is He Saying Those Terrible Things About Me?* A "Monologue Profile Reference Chart" is provided on pages 203–219 to help you quickly locate the material you want.

Finally, we hope these monologues will lead actors and fellow film buffs to some of the great pleasures we experienced reading hundreds of screenplays and watching countless movies in preparation for writing this book.

—Marisa Smith
Amy Schewel
New York City
January 1986

INTRODUCTION

Film, as everyone knows, is a visual medium. One of the greatest performances by any actress in the history of movies consists of a great beauty doing nothing but staring unblinkingly at the camera as her ship pulls slowly away from the shore. People weep, and THE END appears on the screen. No explanations, no histrionics, not a word of dialogue . . . and certainly no conversation about what she is thinking or feeling. The audience writes its own monologue.

This moment is from Rouben Mamoulian's celebrated 1933 film, *Queen Christina*, starring Greta Garbo. Garbo's face, Mamoulian's direction, William Daniels's cinematography, and Adrian's costumes all contribute to an eloquent film performance . . . a purely visual characterization. Some people might say, "Who needs dialogue for film actors? Who needs a screenwriter?" But the truth is that *Queen Christina*'s authors (H. M. Harwood and Salka Viertel) made their own considerable contributions to that wordless finale. They had created a strong and dramatic woman for Garbo to bring to life, a woman audiences had heard talk, laugh, question, and philosophize for nearly ninety minutes before that final moment in which she says nothing, leaving the viewer to complete her story.

Queen Christina is an example of the collaboration necessary among writers, directors, and actors in film, a relationship of mutual support and interaction, and also a relationship in which each group constantly eliminates and minimalizes the other's contribution, to achieve the effective "less is more" goal of great films. When a writer creates a believable character living in a believable world, the director can eliminate some of the script's dialogue, remove any expository speeches, and translate ideas into action. He can use the medium itself to replace the words with varied locations, rapid manipulation of space, freedom of action, easy change of perspective, close-up views, and much more. Skillful directorial use of the medium enhances the actor's performance, allowing for naturalistic behavior that provides character through the smallest things. Film allows an actor or actress to do practically nothing at all and still give a powerful performance. The more an actor understands this phenomenon of the medium, the more freedom this in turn returns to the screenwriter, who can write simple, everyday speech instead of high-flown rhetoric. He can use a compact, zingy one-liner instead of three pages of eloquent prose. In fact, the history of screenwriting in most people's minds is a long list of famous single lines of dialogue that have become unforgettable. People who are movie fans can easily tell you who said, "I steal," or "Frankly, my dear, I don't give a damn," or "Nobody's perfect," or "What we have here is a failure to communicate." (They can also tell you who did *not* say "Play it again, Sam" or "Come with me to the Casbah.")

This complex interaction of director/writer/actor is sometimes discussed as if the writer were not a part of it. For the past decade or so it has been fashionable to act as if the screenwriter did not write the movie. It also has become fashionable to say, "Films should not talk," or "The mark of the great screenplay is the absence of language." These negative thoughts are not necessarily wrong, but they are misleading. Since people talk, films about people talk. It's not the absence of language that makes a great movie—it's the creative use of the medium with all its possibilities, which include sound and dialogue. The point is not to eliminate dialogue, the actor's tool, but not to rely on it alone to express ideas and feelings. A great screenwriter writes great dialogue, but he also writes an effective absence of dialogue. He creates a character who talks—and who does not always talk. He knows a film performer acts a character partly through what he says, and partly through what he does, where he goes, what he sees. Because the film medium can give the actor so much else with which to build his role, the screen monologue is not a common thing. No screenwriter uses one as his first choice. No director allows one in his movie without thinking twice about it. And no actor expects a great many "to-be-or-not-to-be" speeches in his film career.

This is precisely why a collection of carefully researched and selected film monologues makes a treasure trove of new material for an actor or actress looking for new audition scenes. When you *do* have a monologue in a movie, it sure as heck has to be good to have survived. With everything else going on, and with everyone, including the writer, trying to eliminate it, only the very, very best long speech for an actor will appear in a finished film. The others end up on the cutting-room floor. As Tracy says about Hepburn in *Pat and Mike,* "There's not a lot there, but what's there is cherce." A good movie monologue is an actor's dream.

The Actor's Book of Movie Monologues contains an amazing variety. In reading through the various scenes, I found many excellent ones from films I had not cared for much otherwise, and a series of outstanding ones from favorite movies. On the whole, I preferred the scenes from American films. The idea of a translation of an Ingmar Bergman movie, to be reenacted in English, leaves me cold. Frequently, the movies had left me cold in the first place, but this is obviously a matter of taste. As I read the scenes I thought what an excellent idea this book really is, providing so much original material for auditioners. I wondered why no one had collected such scenes before, and in doing so, I thought of potential problems in using movie scenes out of context.

Obviously, anyone who decides to use a movie monologue for an audition has to remember that films provide a great deal of support for a performer other than just lighting and costuming—cutting to other actors who trigger audience reactions through a particular response, controlled compositions, and camera movements that direct the listener's response and release him from watching only the actor.

And the most obvious problem of all—it's tough to be Jimmy Stewart! Anyone who decides to audition as "Mr. Smith" had better be careful not to conjure up Stewart's image, as he is an eternal, powerful, and overwhelming competitor in the role, easily pictured and remembered by the auditioners.

Setting these minor warnings aside, I would say that this book contains some of the very best material by American screenwriters in the history of movies, an incredible list of choices for both men and women. There are scenes that represent a turning point, or pivotal moment, in a character's life, as when Mr. Chips says farewell (*Goodbye, Mr. Chips*) or when Joanna says she will give up her son (*Kramer vs. Kramer*). There are powerful scenes of persuasion and statements of personal philosophies from films as varied as *Mr. Smith Goes to Washington*, *Adam's Rib*, and *To Kill a Mockingbird*. There are warnings about the future from realistic, down-to-earth people such as Tom Joad in *The Grapes of Wrath*, but also from imaginary creatures like the spaceman in *The Day the Earth Stood Still*; discussions from troubled characters about their innermost feelings, as in *The Conversation* and *Last Tango in Paris*; seduction scenes from the teasing (Delores in *In the Heat of the Night*), the rough and half comic (Charlie Allnutt in *The African Queen*), and the overt all-American hard-sell (Shapeley in *It Happened One Night*). I particularly like a unique section, chosen with imagination and insight, in which a single character assumes several roles for different purposes, as in *Next Stop, Greenwich Village* (to play out a movie-star fantasy), and *The Big Chill* (to be both a talk-show host and the guest, as a way of exorcising self-loathing and disappointment).

In terms of technique, the actor's job in film is somewhat different than in theater. The stage actor must reach out from himself, projecting subtlety as far as the very last row in the very top balcony. The film actor, on the other hand, must draw in, pulling people out of their seats toward himself, into his character, up onto the screen. (Pity the poor players who reverse the process—the false and bombastic film actor, or the timid stage performer who can't be heard.) However, on the bottom line, an actor's job is the same in all forms—to communicate, to create a real character, and to be honest in the performance. His tools are the same in any medium—voice, body, gesture—and his responders are also the same—the eternal, waiting audience. Today, actors and actresses make their livings on the stage, and also in film, video, and television, so materials from all sources should be pressed into service. A book like this is not only fun for people who like movies just to read; it's a useful, practical, challenging work tool for performers. And think about this: More people have probably watched *Mr. Smith Goes to Washington* in the past year than have gone to a production of *Hamlet* in the past ten. This doesn't downplay "to be or not to be," but it does suggest that what Mr. Smith has to say is every bit as meaningful, as powerful, as moving, as entertaining, and as challenging to hear performed as anything else ever written for actors.

Jeanine Basinger
Professor of Film Studies and Curator of the
Wesleyan Cinema Archives, Wesleyan University
October 29, 1985

INTERVIEW
with Nikos Psacharopoulos
Artistic and Executive Director
Williamstown Theatre Festival

Conducted by Marisa Smith and Amy Schewel

Q: What advice would you give an actor who is selecting, preparing, and performing a monologue for an audition?

NP: A lot depends on what the person is preparing the audition for. There are auditions that are prepared for the "commercial world," meaning strictly for somebody to get a job. So, if the person is doing the monologue to get a job, he should know one important thing: what the director, or the agent, or manager really wants or likes. There are directors who love and fall for energy, or sincerity, or character, and the same is true, of course, of the agents and the producers. I would say that the most important thing, since this is something practical rather than soul-searching, is to know what the market is.

On the other hand, I find it very strange for somebody doing an audition to readjust chairs, bring props out of their bags, and all of that, because on a first audition I'm only looking for honest acting—acting where people connect to themselves. That's all I want. Everything else will come later. A person doing an audition should choose something that's very close to themselves. They should play their own age, their own background, and, more important, their own emotional quality or something that they really connect with.

Q: What about the preparation of the monologue, before the actor comes in and does it?

NP: Again it is so tough, because I know that there are a lot of agents who are interested in some kind of *flair*. If you're going to do, let's say, an audition for ACT [American Conservatory Theatre in San Francisco], where they're doing a lot of stylish material, such as Feydeau and Rostand and so on, you want one kind of audition. But for directors like Austin Pendleton or Arvin Brown or any of the people who want to see some kind of emotional world of the actor, you do another.

Q: What about you? When someone comes in to do an audition, what do you like to see?

NP: Well, again it all depends on what the audition is for. For a class I like to see somebody who is "working," who's making the audition a process rather than a result. It doesn't show me what the person *is* but what they can *do*. It's just like doing scales, emotional scales—the way a singer would come and sing a few notes; I don't really worry about the melody. I don't really worry about the interpretation of the play. Now, there are some directors who love to have an interpretation, saving them from really having to make this kind of judgment. Unfortunately, too many times directors love to have choices made by actors, because then *they* don't have to make choices. I basically believe I can make any choice I want to for an actor; I just want actors to do them well. If, in an audition, somebody wants to do Hamlet as a comedy or as a drama or as a tragedy or as a melodrama, I don't really care. I only care about how they use their emotional, vocal, and physical equipment, and if those three things go together. I also want to see if somebody is especially vocal or especially emotional—if one side of them is stonger or weaker than the other side.

Q: Do actors ever do things at an audition that particularly turn you off?

NP: Yes, I think somebody must have told actors that being efficient is great. They change shirts and open bags and move chairs and readjust—all these things that are totally unnecessary. Also, they like telling you things. For example, someone comes to an audition and says, "This is a speech from *Hot L Baltimore*, and as you know, *Hot L Baltimore* was written by . . ." or "This is *Saint Joan*, and Saint Joan was a soldier . . ." and so on. This information doesn't really matter, because most of the time a work of art is or should be self-explanatory. I love it when an actor gives no commentary; I love somebody to come in and do it with a sense of . . . not a sense of efficiency, but a sense of proportion, to just stand up there and use themselves in the best possible way.

Q: Can you think of any particularly memorable auditions?

NP: When Frank Langella came to audition for me, he did four lines, and I cut him off and said, "Great." He said, "What do you mean? I prepared—" And I said, "Listen, I'm going to hire you." At that time he hadn't done anything, but after his four lines from *Richard II* I knew I wanted to use him. Olympia Dukakis did the same, a very brief audition. I was very impressed with the way they were using themselves. I hired Blythe Danner on that basis too. I saw a clip from a movie that was maybe one minute long or less. That's all I ever saw of her. But what I saw was an honesty, an honest use of her wonderful instrument. What else do you need? Someone who's a great singer can sing five notes for you and you take a chance.

I think actors torture themselves too much by confusing acting and the acting instrument with decisions. I'm not saying people should not think, but I just believe you should not be obvious. You often don't really know with a great painting or sculpture what the exact thought is, because the piece of art has to be stronger than the artist.

When I see that actors are in the process of discovery, that's "working." Peter Brook has an example of somebody going into a cave, an archaeologist, and first they find the legs of a horse. Then they might find the neck and so on. They don't go into the cave saying, "First I find this, then

I find that, then I put it all together and have a horse."
You find things, and then *eventually* you put them together.
And that's what the actor should really do.

Q: Do you think the actor should make any intellectual
decisions before he goes through the process of discovery?

NP: The real question is how well the actor has learned
to give himself permission to use the acting equipment—
his emotional world, his voice, his body, his attitude. If
you don't do this, you're in trouble. Again, I'm not saying
that actors should not think. All I'm saying is that if thought
made us great artists, we'd all be Picassos. You've got to
be able to play the instrument first, before you are an artist.
If you play that instrument in a certain kind of way, then,
of course, you become a different kind of artist. But the
point is, you can't just say that because you *think*, because
your thoughts are great and your perception of the material
is great, you're an artist. You're not. It is the emotional
and the physical response that is important, which obviously is based on an intellectual world. Most of the people
I work with are really very bright. That's not what I'm
talking about. I think acting is like the great *Saint Joan*
line, "I hear my voices first and I find reasons for them
afterwards."

Q: With a monologue, how would you advise an actor
to approach all those words?

NP: First, make the other imaginary person on stage
real. The most decisive element of acting is really *re*acting,
right? So, until you visualize that other person, or those
other people, forget it. You cannot do a monologue. Second, which is more interesting in terms of movies, remember that the camera has many functions. With the good
directors the camera is part of what we perceive as the
actor's behavior. The camera spells behavior itself. The
director makes a judgment: Is this a two-shot, or a one-
shot, or a crowd shot—do you move in, do you cut, do you

dissolve? The good directors—not everybody, but the really good ones—use these techniques as behavior. As an actor, you have the advantage of doing what the cameraman does. You do it with a certain kind of emotional emphasis and certain technical emphasis in the work. Often, in movies, the camera takes over. Sometimes the music takes over. But what can happen with a movie monologue is that you take the music out of the monologue and put it into the acting. I think this is fascinating.

Q: In all the many plays that you've worked on, have there been certain monologues that you remember?

NP: Chekhov monologues are spectacular. What really makes a good monologue, such as one by Shakespeare or Chekhov, is that there is a moment of a certain intensity which becomes personal and transcends the public event. So, if Hamlet is going to say, "To be or not to be," if he is going to ask, "Do I kill myself or don't I kill myself," he has to do it alone, right? There's no way around it. If the doctor in *Three Sisters* has to say, "I killed somebody on the operating table," he has to do that alone. If people are around, they might not even understand. That's true in all the great Chekhov monologues; Ranevska talks to Trefimov; Andre talks to the old deaf man that comes from the town council, who might as well not be there, because he doesn't "hear." In Gorky's *Enemies* there is a great speech that the actress has, one of the greatest monologues in the history of the theater, which is delivered to a drunk husband who is more or less out of it. So, the greatest monologues are moments when the sense of privacy becomes public. Those are the moments in theater when a playwright allows himself to go overboard. All the great actors have made their private worlds public, and that's the difference between a good actor and a bad actor. That's all it is—giving themselves permission to appear to be silly and ridiculous and emotional and human and glorious.

I am not trying to find actors to justify the material. I'm trying to find actors. I *assume* that every actor does something different. I *assume* that if I need them as actors, I will use them as actors; but when I direct a particular play, *I* will help them shape the role.

When doing a monologue, you should know what happened before. This is going to be the springboard of the speech, but it is not the full context. I call this "time-given circumstances," which has its own depth before the speech. For example, Saint Joan can't immediately say, "They told me you were fools." She has been sitting there for a long, long time listening to these people talk. Now, that is the context, but if you're an actor doing *Saint Joan,* you approach the scene from the feeling that, "I've been sitting, and I've been waiting, and I've been waiting, and I've been waiting, and I've been waiting." And it's finally built. So, what happens? There is a tricky way of doing it for interpretation or for doing it through your soul. Good actors don't use time-given circumstances for the interpretation. Good actors always use it to really get going. That's why it is so very wonderful to work with a very good actor. Blythe Danner, no matter what the situation, turns time-given circumstances into an advantage for her acting. Everything is a springboard for her to be fuller as an actress. You could say, "Oh, let's not see the scene *this* way, let's see it *that* way," but she would still use either direction as a springboard, though a different kind of springboard each time. If you can use the circumstances as a springboard rather than as a corset, you're okay. They will not limit you; they should give you freedom, the freedom to work.

Q: How do you feel about the phrase "becoming a character"?

NP: I don't know what that means, really. A lot of people talk about becoming a character, but I wonder if character simply exists or if character is what you do. If somebody has six things to do, why do they worry about being a character? It's the six things that they do, and that becomes the character.

Q: *Character* is a word that is frequently thrown around.

NP: It's like all theatrical terms. Anytime somebody translates one form into another, you're in trouble. It's like food critics trying to find an accurate word to describe a meal, which is difficult, because it's a taste. This constant need to define the art world with words is very problematic. I never know what people mean. I only know what I see and what I hear. And that's why I think you can't really write a textbook about acting. The easiest way of showing something about acting is to use a videotape. With a tape you see what is happening. Then you can make some comments as the director or as a teacher and see the tape again.

Q: Do you ever begin to see actors as the characters they are playing rather than as themselves?

NP: I don't find that a useful distinction, because it's never really interesting to see somebody as Blanche in *A Streetcar Named Desire*. It's never interesting to see four apples. It is only interesting to see Cézanne's apples. Or somebody else's apples. With Blanche, it's interesting to see Diane Wiest's Blanche versus, let's say, Carrie Nye's. One bad thing about acting is that people assume there is somehow, somewhere, an archetype, a goal for each character in a play. That's not interesting. That's why we don't watch much theater nowadays. People don't realize that in an ideal world people should see six actors' Hamlets.

What's great about good actors is that they realize the background of the text and what is underneath the text; they make you believe them. Some actors make the strangest choices, if you think about them. But when you're watching the play or movie, you can't think about them, because the actors are very convincing. But you may go home and say, "Why did he do that?"

A director can just give you the shape. I don't want to know the limitations before I know the possibilities and the potential. So, in the auditions I look for potential. I look for possibilities. I look for lack of discipline, frankly. I love actors who go to their "emotional junkyard," pick up everything, and bring it on stage. Afterward it is up to me to keep things "down." That is my job, to shape rather than to invent. The actor invents. So I'd rather see too many things going on and cut them down, trim them to the needs of the material, size and edit them, than see absolutely nothing and then have to pump energy and life into the actors.

I love to see open work, and sometimes I get lucky and see work that is wonderful.

THE
ACTOR'S BOOK
OF
MOVIE
MONOLOGUES

M

Nero Film, 1931
Screenplay by Thea von Harbou, Paul Falkenberg,
Adolf Jansen, and Karl Vash
Directed by Fritz Lang

Time: 1931
Place: A German city
This is based on an actual case in Düsseldorf, Germany. A
psychopathic killer is preying upon young children. Police,
in their frenzy to find and stop this murderer, so saturate
the city streets and underworld alleyways with patrols that
the normal domain of the common criminals and underworld pickpockets, thieves, and beggars is turned upside
down. These everyday street criminals organize themselves
to track down the madman, so things can return to normal
in *their* world of crime.

The band of criminals does trap the killer—by marking
him on the back of his coat with the letter *M* for "Murderer." The murderer is cornered in a large cellar, surrounded by the criminals. He is put through an angry mock
trial. They argue over whether he's responsible for what
he did, or if he's insane and should be turned over to
doctors.

One of the criminals shouts: "We want to render you
harmless . . . but you'll only be harmless when you're dead."
The murderer demands to be handed over to the police,
"over to the jurisdiction of the common law." The crowd
laughs and says that they'll never let him go—to be insti-
tutionalized, perhaps escape one day, or be pardoned and
be "free as air . . . protected by the law because of mental
illness . . . off again chasing little girls." No, they say, "You
must disappear." As the angry crowd prepares to deal with
him, the murderer speaks out in his own defense.

3

MURDERER

But I can't help what I do. I can't help it . . . I can't . . .
I can't . . . I can't help it.

(in complete despair)

What do you know about it? What are you saying? If it
comes to that, who are you? What right have you to speak?

(He turns his head to look at them all.)

Who are you . . . All of you? . . . Criminals! Perhaps you're
even proud of yourselves? Proud of being able to break
safes, to climb into buildings or cheat at cards . . . Things
you could just as well keep your fingers off . . . You wouldn't
need to do all that if you had learnt a proper trade . . . or
if you worked. If you weren't a bunch of lazy bastards . . .
But I . . .

(His hands clutch at his chest.)

I can't help myself! I haven't any control over this evil thing
that's inside me—the fire, the voices, the torment.

(agonized)

Always . . . always, there's this evil force inside me . . .
It's there all the time, driving me out to wander through
the streets . . . following me . . . silently, but I can feel it
there . . . It's me, pursuing myself, because . . . I want to
escape . . . to escape from myself . . . but it's impossible.
I can't. I can't escape. I have to obey it. I have to run . . .
run . . . streets . . . endless streets. I want to escape. I
want to get away. And I am pursued by ghosts. Ghosts of
mothers. And of those children . . . They never leave me.

(shouting desperately)

They are there, there, always, always. Always . . . except . . . except when I do it . . . when I . . .

*(He raises his hands toward his neck, as
though he were about to strangle a victim,
then he lets them fall limp at his sides.)*

Then I can't remember anything . . . And afterwards I see

those posters and I read what I've done . . . I read . . .
and . . . and read . . . Did I do that? But I can't remember
anything about it . . . But who will believe me? Who knows
what it feels like to be me? How I'm forced to act . . .

(His eyes close in ecstasy.)

How I must . . . Don't want to, but must . . .

(He screams.)

Must . . . Don't want to . . . must. And then . . . a voice
screams . . . I can't bear to hear it.

(He throws himself against the wooden barrier
in a paroxysm, covering his ears with his
hands, at the height of his fit.)

I can't . . . I can't go on. Can't go on . . . Can't go on . . .
Can't go on . . .

I Am a Fugitive from a Chain Gang

Warner Brothers (Produced by Hal B. Wallis), 1932
Screenplay by Sheridan Gibney, Brown Holmes,
and Robert E. Burns
Directed by Mervyn LeRoy

Time: Post–World War I
Place: Small town, U.S.A.

James Allen, a young factory worker from a small town, is
back from the war. An ex-military man now with ambitions,
he vows never to return to the drudgery of factory labor.
He wants to try construction work but can't find a job. He
falls in with the wrong group of people and through unlucky
circumstances is at the scene of a robbery and is manipu-
lated into participating. He's arrested and sentenced to five
years on a chain gang.

The conditions at the convict camps are deplorable. The

prisoners are ruled by sadistic camp wardens and guards. James escapes, tries to build his life again, but is betrayed and must return to the prison camp. He escapes again but is captured, and this time his spirit is broken.

In the beginning of the film James is just back from the war and eager to convince his mother and brother of the value of his ambitions.

ALLEN

. . . It's all up here . . .
(Tapping his head, he looks tenderly at his mother, who is shocked.)
I told you about it when I first came home.
(with vehemence)
This isn't the kind of work I want to do . . . It's too monotonous! The whole factory's monotonous! Sometimes I feel I'd like to jump right out of my skin.
(plaintively)
I've simply got to get out of it—and get some kind of an engineering job—like I wanted to do in the first place.
(He looks at his MOTHER, hoping she will understand. She looks at him with a world of devotion; she shakes her head, sorry for him. The BROTHER sighs impatiently. He has feared that this subject would be brought up again. He crosses to ALLEN.)
[BROTHER
(to ALLEN)
You don't seem to realize—]
ALLEN
(interrupting)
That's it—realize! No one seems to realize that I am different now than when I went away. I have changed! I have seen things! I have been through hell! Here folks are con-

cerned about my uniform—how I dance—I am out of step with everybody—all the while I was hoping to come back and start a new life—to be free—and again I find myself under orders—a drab routine—cramped, mechanical, even worse than the army and YOU—

(*pointing to his BROTHER*)

—all of you trying your darnedest to map out my future— to harness me and lead me around to do what YOU think is best for ME! It doesn't occur to you that I have grown in mind and body—that I have learned that life is more important than a medal on my chest or a stupid, insignificant job! This town is stifling me—I've got to get out of it! I want to work, do things! Try to become something more than just a clock puncher in a small-town shoe factory!

It Happened One Night

Columbia Pictures (Produced by Frank Capra), 1934
Screenplay by Robert Riskin
Based on the story "Night-Bus," by Samuel Hopkins Adams
Directed by Frank Capra

Time: 1934
Place: A bus, on the road between Miami and New York City
In this romantic comedy, Peter Warne, an experienced newspaper reporter, meets Ellie Andrews, a young heiress. Spoiled, willful, and rich, Ellie has just jumped off her father's yacht to escape her impending wedding to her stuffy fiancé. Her father posts a cash reward for anyone who finds his daughter, and the tabloids are full of the story and the search.

Peter stumbles upon Ellie, and, recognizing the opportunity she presents, pretends not to know who she is. He intends to travel with her, befriend her, and get the hot story. Out of money, her suitcase lost, Ellie sees no alternative but to depend on Peter to guide her to New York City.

As they hitchhike across the countryside, staying at run-down motels and camping under the stars, their testy and combative relationship begins to develop into romance.

At one point at the beginning of their journey, Ellie and Peter hop a bus. Avoiding Peter, Ellie happens to find herself seated next to a traveling office-supplies salesman named Shapeley. After a slow, lascivious gaze at Ellie's ankles, calves, knees, then pretty face, Shapeley begins to make his move.

SHAPELEY

Hi, sister— All alone? My name's Shapeley. Might as well get acquainted. It's gonna be a long trip—gets tiresome later on. Specially for somebody like you. You look like you got class.

(on his breath)

Yessir! With a capital K.

(chuckles at his own sally)

And I'm a guy that knows class when he sees it, believe you me. Ask any of the boys. They'll tell you. Shapeley sure knows how to pick 'em. Yessir. Shapeley's the name, and that's the way I like 'em. You made no mistake sitting next to me.

(confidentially)

Just between us, the kinda muggs you meet on a hop like this ain't nothin' to write home to the wife about. You gotta be awful careful who you hit it up with, is what I always say, and you can't be too particular, neither. Once when I was comin' through North Carolina, I got to gabbin' with a good-lookin' mama. One of those young ones, you know, and plenty classy, too. Kinda struck my fancy. You know how it is. Well, sir, you coulda' knocked me over with a Mack truck. I was just warming up when she's yanked offa the bus. Who do you think she was? Huh? Might as well give up. The girl bandit! The one the papers been writin' about.

(awed by the recollection)
Yessir, you coulda knocked me over with a Mack truck.
(He pulls out a cigar, lights it, takes a vigorous puff, turns to her again.)
What's the matter, sister? You ain't sayin' much.
Looks like you're one up on me. Nothin' I like better than to meet a high-class mama that can snap 'em back at you. 'Cause the colder they are, the hotter they get, is what I always say. Take this last town I was in. I run into a dame— not a bad looker, either—but boy, was she an iceberg! Every time I opened my kisser, she pulls a ten strike on me. It sure looked like cold turkey for old man Shapeley. I sell office supplies, see? And this hotsy-totsy lays the damper on me quick. She don't need a thing—and if she did she wouldn't buy it from a fresh mugg like me. Well, says I to myself—Shapeley, you better go to work. You're up against a lulu. Well, I'm here to tell you, sister, I opened up a line of fast chatter that had that dame spinnin' like a Russian dancer. Before I got through she bought enough stuff to last the firm a year. And did she put on an act when I blew town!

(ELLIE has scarcely listened to him, and has divided her attention between glancing back at PETER and staring at SHAPELEY as if he were insane. None of which bothers SHAPELEY. He goes on with his merry chatter, blowing rings of smoke in the direction of the ceiling.)

Yessir. When a cold mama gets hot—boy, how she sizzles!
She kinda cramped my style, though. I didn't look at a
dame for three towns.

>   (*quickly*)

Not that I couldn't. For me it's always a cinch. I got a much
better chance than the local talent.

>   (*confidentially*)

You see, they're kinda leery about the local talent. Too
close to home. Know what I mean?

>   (*She has now reached the point where she*
>   *could, without any compunction, strangle him.*)

But take a bird like me—it's here today—and gone tomorrow. And what happens is nobody's business.

>   (*She turns helplessly to PETER, off screen. He*
>   *is apparently oblivious of her presence.*)

But I don't go in for that kinda stuff—much. I like to pick
my fillies. Take you, for instance. You're my type. No kiddin', sister. I could go for you in a big way. "Fun-on-the-
side Shapeley" they call me, and the accent's on the fun,
believe you me.

Mutiny on the Bounty

MGM (Produced by Irving Thalberg and Albert Lewin), 1935
Screenplay by Talbot Jennings, Jules Furthman,
and Carey Wilson
Based on the novel by Charles Nordhoff and James Hall
Directed by Frank Lloyd

Time: 1792
Place: England
Roger Byam, a man from the upper class in his twenties,
sets off on the H.M.S. *Bounty* in 1787, bound for Tahiti

and intending to carry on the family seafaring tradition. The captain of the *Bounty*, Bligh, proves brutal and murderous, and ultimately Byam winds up below deck in chains. The captain's first mate and antagonist on the voyage, Fletcher Christian, leads a mutiny. He and his men put Bligh and those who are loyal to him asea in a longboat. Byam, sensitive to the injustices of Bligh but unsympathetic to the mutiny, wishes to join the "loyalists." However, by the time he is released from his chains and emerges from below deck, the longboat is full and departs without him.

Bligh succeeds in reaching England, returns in another ship, and captures some of the mutineers, including Byam. They are brought to Portsmouth and court-martialed. After the court martial's deliberations, Byam is returned to the courtroom. He sees a sword pointed toward him, a sign that the verdict is guilty. The judge offers him the opportunity to speak his last. Later, Byam is acquitted.

(*Note:* When Byam mentions the "ten coconuts and two cheeses," he's referring to food that Bligh stole.)

BYAM

My lord, much as I desire to live, I'm not afraid to die. Since I first sailed on the *Bounty*, over four years ago, I've known how men can be made to suffer worse things than death. Cruelty, beyond duty, beyond necessity.

(*to BLIGH*)

Captain Bligh, you've told your story of mutiny on the *Bounty*, how men plotted against you. Seized your ship, cast you adrift in an open boat. A great venture in science brought to nothing, two British ships lost.

(*BYAM looks left and then to foreground as he speaks.*)

But there's another story, Captain Bligh, of ten coconuts and two cheeses. The story of a man who robbed his sea-

men, cursed them, flogged them, not to punish but to break
their spirit.

(to COURT)

A story of greed and tyranny and of anger against it! Of
what it cost! One man, my lord, would not endure such
tyranny. That's why you hounded him, that's why you hate
him, hate his friends. And that's why you're beaten. Fletcher
Christian is still free. But Christian lost, too, my lord. God
knows he's judged himself . . . more harshly than you could
judge him. I say to his Father, he was my friend. No finer
man ever lived. I don't try to justify his crime, his mutiny.
But I condemn the tyranny that drove him to it. I don't
speak here for myself alone, nor for these men you've condemned. I speak in their names, in Fletcher Christian's
name, for all men at sea. These men don't ask for comfort,
they don't ask for safety! If they could speak to you they'd
say: Let us choose to do our duty willingly, not the choice
of a slave, but the choice of free English men. They ask
only freedom that England expects for every man. Oh, if
one man among you believed that. One man! He could
command the fleets of England, he could sweep the seas
for England. If he called his men to duty, not by flaying
their backs, but by lifting their hearts! That's all . . .

Mr. Deeds Goes to Town

Columbia Pictures (Produced by Frank Capra), 1936
Screenplay by Robert Riskin
Based on the story "Opera Hat," by Clarence Budington
Kellard
Directed by Frank Capra

Time: 1936
Place: New York City
Longfellow Deeds, a simple small-town citizen, is advised one day that he has inherited $20 million. Suddenly one of the country's richest men, Deeds travels to New York, where his inheritance is to be handled. Terribly naive, he becomes the target of headline-hungry newspapermen and a collection of crooked relatives and acquaintances scheming to wrest the money from him.

Babe, a pretty but tough newspaperwoman, is promised great rewards by her editor if she can get the inside track with Deeds. She manages to slip inside his guard, and they ostensibly fall in love. But, unbeknownst to Deeds, Babe is writing sensationalistic articles about him for her newspaper, dubbing him "Cinderella Man."

The pressure in New York begins to get to Deeds, and his eventual discovery of Babe's duplicity depresses him. So, after a chance encounter with a poor man, he decides to give all his inheritance to the needy. This brash decision, combined with other eccentricities on Deeds's part, creates a wonderful opportunity for the group conspiring to get Deeds's money: They bring him to trial on insanity charges.

At the trial Deeds is so depressed and disillusioned, he won't even speak in his own defense. He is about to be convicted when Babe, by now deeply in love with Deeds and horribly guilty over her treachery, jumps up and addresses the courtroom.

BABE
(to JUDGE)

No! No! Wait a minute! You can't do it! Please—you've got to make him talk.

(to LONGFELLOW, pleading softly)

Darling, please—I know everything I've done. I know how horrible I've been. If you never see me again—no matter what happens—do this for me.

(to JUDGE, frantically)

You said I could speak! You said I could have my say if I were rational. I'm rational! I'll take the witness chair. He must be made to defend himself before you arrive at a decision. I know *why* he won't defend himself! *That* has a bearing on the case! He's been hurt! He's been hurt by everybody he's met since he came. Principally by me. He's been the victim of every conniving crook in town. The newspapers pounced on him—made him a target for their feeble humor. I was smarter than the rest of them! I got closer to him so that I could laugh louder. Why shouldn't he keep quiet? Every time he said anything it was twisted around to sound imbecilic. He can thank me for it! I handed the gang a great laugh. This is a fitting climax to my sense of humor. Certainly I wrote those articles. I was going to get a raise—and a month's vacation! But I stopped writing them when I found out what he was all about! When I realized how real he was—when I found out he could never fit in with our distorted viewpoint—because *his* was honest and sincere and good. If that man is crazy, Your Honor, the rest of us belong in straitjackets.

Things to Come

London Films (Produced by Alexander Korda), 1936
Screenplay by H. G. Wells
Based on his book *The Shape of Things to Come*
Directed by William Cameron Menzies

Time: The future, beginning in 1936 and looking ahead to
the 1940s and on to 2059
Place: Earth
This film is the story of John Cabal, an aviator, and his
descendants. Cabal lives through a predicted series of terrible wars, epidemics, and destruction from 1940 to 1970.

At war's end Cabal becomes the leader of a new society
of scientists, scholars, and inventors who are committed to
rebuilding civilization. This group attempts to quell the last
warring pockets on the earth.

In 1970, Cabal flies an airplane to one of these areas. In
this unenlightened district Cabal is seized when he lands
and is taken to a prison cell at the instruction of the "Boss"
of the region. While waiting to meet the "Boss," Cabal is
visited by Roxana, a beautiful woman in her twenties who
relishes risk and adventure, in love and in life. She is curious to see this man from "another world" with another
way of thinking. She speaks to Cabal.

ROXANA
You know—I am not a stupid woman.
[CABAL
I am sure.]
ROXANA
This life here—is limited. War—rich plunder. Shining prizes.
Of a sort. War always going on and never ending. Flags.
Marching. I adore the Chief. I've always adored him since

he took control in the Pestilence Days when everyone else lost heart. He rules. He is firm. Everyone—every woman finds him strong and attractive. I can't complain. I have everything that is to be had here. But—This is a small limited world we live in here. *You* bring in the breath of something greater. When I saw you swooping down out of the sky—when I saw you march into the Town Hall—I felt: This man lives in a greater world. And you spoke of the Mediterranean and the East, and your camps and factories. I've read about the Mediterranean and Greece and Egypt and India. I can read—a lot of those old books. I'm not like most of the younger people. I learnt a lot before education stopped and the schools closed down. I want to see that world away there. Sunshine, palms, snowy mountains, blue seas.

[CABAL

If I had my way—you might fly to all that in a couple of days.]

(ROXANA becomes pensive and looks down.)

ROXANA

If you were free . . . And if I was free. I don't think any man has ever understood any woman since the beginning of things. You don't understand our imaginations. How wild our imaginations can be. I wish I were a man.

(She stands up abruptly.)

Oh if I were a man! . . . Does any man realise what the life of a woman is? How trivial we *have* to be. We have to please. We are obliged to please. If we attempt to take a serious share in life, are we welcomed? And all the while—. Men are so self-satisfied, so blind, so limited. . . . I see things happening here—! Injustice. Cruelty. There are things I would do for the poor—things I would do to make things better. I am not allowed. I have to pretend to be eaten up by my dresses, my jewels, my vanities. I make myself beautiful often with an aching heart. . . . But I'm talking about myself. Tell me about yourself—about that greater world you live in. Are *you* a Boss? You have the manner of one who commands. You are sure of yourself. You make me afraid of you. Of the people you come from. Of what you are. Before you came I felt safe here. I felt— things were going on as they have been going on. . . . Always. . . . No hope of change. . . . *Now*—it's all different. What are you people trying to do to us? What do you mean to do to this Boss of mine?

The Life of Emile Zola

Warner Brothers (Produced by Henry Blanke), 1937
Screenplay by Norman Reilly Raine
Based on a story by Heinz Herald and Geza Herczeg
Directed by William Dieterle

Time: 1890s
Place: Paris, France
Emile Zola has risen from years of poverty as a struggling writer and is enjoying great wealth and honor in his later years. He is France's foremost man of letters and is known for championing humanitarian causes and bringing to light, through his writing and activities, the condition of the oppressed and misunderstood.

After the Franco-Prussian Wars, just before the turn of the twentieth century, France is in a chaotic political state. When it is discovered that military secrets have been passed to the Prussians, the general staff of the army frames, court-martials, and convicts a senior officer, Alfred Dreyfus, a Jew, for the crime. He is sent to Devil's Island. Subsequently the real traitor, Count Esterhazy, is discovered and court-martialed. The general staff, the war minister, and others involved in the Dreyfus affair conspire to acquit Esterhazy.

Shortly thereafter, Dreyfus's wife, Lucie, arrives uninvited to the sumptuous house of Zola. She brings documentation of the frame-up of her husband and pleads that Zola bring the matter to the attention of France. Zola refuses, citing his contentment with his life of ease and the danger of possible libel suits against him. Ultimately he weakens and spends the entire night writing on Dreyfus's behalf.

Monologue One. The morning after his visit from Lucie Dreyfus, Zola calls together his editor and other allies, as well as Madame Dreyfus, to the offices of the newspaper *Aurore*. He speaks to those assembled.

Monologue Two. Later in the film Zola is tried for libel. During the trial, which he has willingly called upon himself in order to revive the Dreyfus affair, Zola is subjected to the courtroom of a judge who is partial to Zola's opponents. Lucie Dreyfus is not permitted to testify at length. Labari, Zola's attorney, is cut short during his most promising lines of defense, and the prosecution is allowed to speak virtually at will. Finally Zola speaks on his own behalf. When asked by the assembled what he was up to, Zola replies, "I'm going to explode a bomb!" and begins reading his letter to be published in the newspaper *Aurore*.

Zola was convicted of libel by a jury whose homes in Paris were marked with white X's in case they gave the wrong verdict. The sentence was one year's imprisonment and a fine. Zola fled to England. Soon after, a new Minister of War reopened the issue. The truth came out, Dreyfus was freed and reinstated with honors, and Zola came home to France.

Monologue One

ZOLA

Mr. President of the Republic . . . Permit me to tell you that your record, without blame so far, is threatened with a most shameful blot—this abominable Dreyfus affair . . . ! A court martial has recently, by order, dared to acquit one Esterhazy—a supreme slap at all truth—all justice! But since they have dared, I, too, shall dare! I shall tell the truth, because if I did not, my nights would be haunted by the spectre of an innocent being, expiating, under the most frightful torture, a crime he never committed! It is impossible for honest people to read the iniquitous bill of accusation against Dreyfus without being overcome with indignation and crying out their revulsion. Dreyfus knows several languages—crime! He works hard—crime! No compromising papers are found in his apartment—crime! He goes occasionally to the country of his origin—crime! He endeavors to learn everything—crime! He is not easily worried—crime! He is easily worried—crime! The Minister of War, the Chief of the General Staff, and the Assistant Chief never doubted that the famous bordereau was written by Esterhazy! But the condemnation of Esterhazy involved the revision of the Dreyfus verdict—and that the General Staff wished to avoid at all cost! For over a year the Minister of War and the General Staff have known that Dreyfus is innocent, but they have kept this knowledge to themselves. And those men sleep and they have wives and children they love! Dreyfus cannot be vindicated without condemning the whole General Staff. That is why the General Staff has screened Esterhazy . . . to demolish Dreyfus once more. Such then, Mr. President, is the simple truth!

It is a fearful truth! But, I affirm with intense conviction—
Truth is on the march—and nothing will stop her! Mr.
President, it is time to conclude. I accuse Colonel Dort of
having been the diabolical agent of the affair, and of continuing to defend his deadly work through three years of
revolving machinations! I accuse the Minister of War of
having concealed proofs of the innocence of Dreyfus! I accuse the Chief of Staff and the Assistant Chief of Staff of
being accomplices in the same crime! I accuse the Commander of the Paris garrison of the most monstrous par-
tiality! I accuse the handwriting experts—Messieurs
Belhomme, Varinard and Covart—of having made lying
and fraudulent reports. I accuse the War Office of having
vilely led a campaign to misdirect public opinion and cover
up its sins! I accuse the first court martial of violating all
human rights in condemning a prisoner on testimony kept
secret from him . . . And I accuse the Esterhazy court martial of having covered up this illegality by order, thus com-
mitting in turn the judicial crime of acquitting a guilty man!
In making these accusations, I am aware that I render myself open to prosecution for libel. But that does not matter.
The action I take is designed only to hasten the explosion
of truth and justice. Let there be a trial in the full light of
day!

Monologue Two

ZOLA

Gentlemen . . . In the House of Deputies, a month ago,
to frantic applause, the Prime Minister, Monsieur Meline,
declared that he had confidence in you twelve citizens, into
whose hands he had bestowed the defense of the Army. In
other words, you were being instructed *by order*, to condemn *me*, just as, in that other case the Minister of War
dictated the acquittal of Esterhazy!

(firing up)

His words made his intention to coerce Justice unmistakable! And I denounce them to the consciences of honest men!

(again quietly)

However, my profession is writing—not talking. But from my struggling youth until today, my principal aim has been to strive for truth. That is why I entered this fight! All my friends have told me that it was insane for a single person to oppose the immense machinery of the Law . . . the glory of the Army, and the power of the State.

(after a pause)

They warned me that my actions would be mercilessly crushed . . . that I would be destroyed! But what does it matter if an individual is shattered, if only Justice is resurrected? It has been said that the State summoned me to this Court. That is not true. I am here because *I* wished it! *I alone* have chosen you as my judges! *I alone* decided that this abominable affair should see the light so that France might at last know all and voice her opinion! My act has no other object—my person is of no account. I am satisfied!

(leaning earnestly forward)

But my confidence in you was not shared by the State. They did not dare say all about the whole, undividable affair, and submit it to your verdict. That is no fault of mine. You saw for yourselves how my defense was incessantly silenced.

(with emotion)

Gentlemen—I know you! You are the heart, and the intellect, of my beloved Paris where I was born, and which I have studied for forty years. I see you with your families under the evening lamp . . . I accompany you into your factories—your shops. You are all workers—and righteous men! You will *not* say, like many: "What does it matter if an innocent man is undergoing torture on Devil's Island?

Is the suffering of one obscure person worth the disturbance of a great country?" Perhaps, though, you have been told that by punishing me you will stop a campaign that is injurious to France. Gentlemen, if that *is* your idea, you are mistaken! Look at me! Have I the look of a hireling—a liar—a traitor? I am only a free writer who has given his life to work, and who will resume it tomorrow. Tremendous pressure has been put upon you. "Save the Army! Convict Zola and save France!" I say to you—*pick up the challenge!* Save the Army! And save France! But do it by letting Truth conquer! Not only is an innocent man crying out for justice; but more—much more—a great nation is in desperate danger of forfeiting her honor! So do not take upon yourselves a fault, the burden of which you will forever bear in history! A judicial blunder has been committed. The condemnation of an innocent man induced the acquittal of a guilty man . . . and now today you are asked to condemn me because I rebelled on seeing our country embarked on this terrible course.

(with impassioned plea)

At this solemn moment, in the presence of this tribunal which is the representative of human justice, before you, gentlemen of the jury, before France, before the whole world—I swear that Dreyfus is innocent! By my forty years of work, by all that I have won, by all that I have written to spread the spirit of France, I swear that Dreyfus is innocent! May all that melt away—may my name perish—if Dreyfus be not innocent! *He is innocent!*

Drums Along the Mohawk

Twentieth Century-Fox (Produced by Raymond Griffith),
1939
Screenplay by Lamar Trotti and Sonya Levien
Based on the novel by Walter Edmonds
Directed by John Ford

Time: Revolutionary War
Place: Mohawk Valley, New York State
What is now upstate New York was, at the time of the
American Revolutionary War, part of the western frontier.
A young couple, Gil and Lana Martin, recently married,
set off for Gil's outpost settlement in a horse-drawn wagon.
Lana is from a prosperous city family. Gil is committed to
a pioneer's life and has been living on the frontier with a
trusted older American Indian as his guide and adviser.

Lana must adjust to the hardships and strong-willed settlers of the frontier, but her love for Gil is sure. Together
they fight for the land they've claimed and for their way of
life. They want peace—to build a farm and raise a family.

The Martins and their fellow settlers have to fight not
only British troops and loyalist settlers, but the Indians as
well, who are raiding the pioneer homesteads.

At this point Gil, wounded and delirious, has stumbled
back from a battle. Lana is at his bedside, tending his
wounds and waiting out his fever.

———

GIL
(*in a low toneless voice*)
I remember thinking how hot it was and wondering how
long we'd be away—when it happened . . . I heard a crack—
like a stick breaking—and all of a sudden the fellow next
to me stopped talking and fell over—on his side . . .

(He winces at the pain. LANA mumbles
something. He relaxes again.)
Gɪʟ (cont'd)
(staring straight up)
Then I heard a whistle—and shots from everywhere—and
somebody yelled we'd been ambushed . . . I saw General
Herkimer slide off his horse and grab his knee—and Amos
Hartman, with his head blown half off . . .
(helpless to resist)
Somebody yelled to me to lay down and then I saw them—
all streaked with paint—yellow and red with every color
and back of them Tories in Green coats . . . I got down
behind a log and aimed at a fellow. He leaped straight up
in the air—and fell, face forward . . . After that, we just
kept shooting—as fast as we could load—for I don't know
how long. Adam Helmer crawled up beside me. His musket'd gone wrong, but he had a spear . . . He kept grinning
and I remember thinking: "He's having a good time. He
likes this! . . ." Pretty soon he pointed off and I saw an
Indian coming toward us—naked. I tried to load, but it
was too late . . . Adam stood up and braced his spear, and
the Indian came down . . .
(shuddering)
I never saw a fellow look so funny—so surprised . . . He
just hung there—his mouth open—looking at us . . . not
saying a word . . .
(with sudden fierceness)
I had to shoot him! . . . It was the only thing I could do!
After a while the regulars came at us with bayonets—and
we stood up . . . I saw Caldwell and a Tory Adam said was
Sir Guy Johnson—and Joseph Brant, the half-breed . . .
For a while it seemed the whole woods were full of 'em.
Then we threw down our muskets and went for them—
with clubs and knives and whatever we could lay our hands
on . . . I had my hatchet and was just going for one of 'em,

when a musket went off—right in front of me. I thought
my whole arm had been torn off . . . I couldn't think of
anything except that I was going to die, and how bad it was
to die out there all by myself. The next thing I knew Adam
had me in his arms, and was pouring brandy down me and
telling me to stop fainting like a girl . . . And he said the
fight was over, and we'd won the battle of Ariskeny . . .
Then it began to rain and I was sick . . .

(sighs heavily)

George Weaver was shot in the groin, and John was bending
over him, crying—and Mark DeMouth was dead . . . And
all this time General Herkimer sat there smoking his pipe
and holding his knee. Then he said we'd better all be going
home . . .

(a long silence)

Out of 600 of us, about 240 were still alive . . .

[LANA

(agonized for him)

My poor Gil, it must have been awful.]

GIL

Yes, but we won. We licked 'em. We showed 'em they
couldn't take this valley.

(looking at her wearily)

Lana—do you hear? We won!

*(He sighs once more, then drops into sleep—
the sleep of utter exhaustion.)*

Mr. Smith Goes to Washington

Columbia Pictures (Produced by Frank Capra), 1939
Screenplay by Sidney Buchman
Based on a story by Lewis R. Foster
Directed by Frank Capra

Time: 1930s, The Depression
Place: Washington, D.C.

One of the senators from a Western state has just died. James Taylor, the political boss of the state, wants the governor to appoint a nonentity for the final two months of the deceased's term of office. Taylor has a plan up his sleeve. A bill containing appropriations for a dam in the state is about to come to the Senate floor. In reality there is no need for a dam. But Taylor and his cronies, who own the land around the proposed dam, stand to profit handsomely by selling it to the state.

Unable to decide on a safe appointee from the cast of local political characters, the governor chooses Jefferson Smith, a small-town Boy Scout leader. Smith goes to Washington. He is very serious-minded and intent on pursuing his position with energy and integrity. Soon after arriving, he hopes to realize a lifelong dream by introducing a bill to create a national summer camp for boys on a piece of land near his hometown. As it turns out, Smith's designated site for the camp lies within the borders of Boss Taylor's proposed dam.

Monologue One. Smith discovers the fraud concerning the dam and wants to stop the bill. When Taylor finds out that Smith knows what's really going on and plans to expose the truth before the Senate, Taylor sends Joseph Paine, the state's senior senator, to tell Smith how the real world of politics works. By coincidence, Paine was a close friend of Jefferson's father, who had been murdered while fighting corruption.

Monologue Two. After Paine's entreaties do not succeed, Boss Taylor attempts to bribe Smith. When Smith turns him down, Taylor and company decide to ruin his reputation. Smith is ridiculed in the Senate and in the press. He fights back by taking the floor in the Senate, intending to filibuster until he has convinced the senators and the country of the rightness of his cause. After two days on his feet, talking nonstop, Smith is ready to collapse. He musters his strength for a final assault.

Monologue One

PAINE
(faltering)
Jeff—I want to talk to you—sit down—
(JEFF remains standing—his eyes fixed on
PAINE.)
Listen, Jeff—you—you don't understand these things—you mustn't condemn me for my part in this without—you've had no experience—you see things as black or white—and a man as angel or devil. That's the young idealist in you. And that isn't how the world runs, Jeff—certainly not Government and politics. It's a question of give and take—you have to play the rules—compromise—you have to leave your ideals outside the door, with your rubbers. I feel I'm the right man for the Senate. And there are certain powers—influence. To stay there, I must respect them. And now and then—for the sake of that power—a dam has to be built—and one must shut his eyes. It's—it's a small compromise. The *best* men have had to make them. Do you understand?

(desperately and with greater emotion as JEFF
is silent)

I know how you feel, Jeff. Thirty years ago—I had those
ideals, too. I was *you*. I had to make the decision you were
asked to make today.

(breaking out)

And I compromised—yes! So that all these years I could
stay in that Senate—and serve the people in a thousand
honest ways! You've got to face facts, Jeff. I've served our
State well, haven't I? We have the lowest unemployment
and the highest Federal grants. But, well, I've had to compromise, had to play ball. You can't count on people voting,
half the time they don't vote, anyway. That's how states
and empires have been built since time began. Don't you
understand? Well, Jeff, you can take my word for it, that's
how things are. Now, I've told you all this because—well,
I've grown very fond of you—about like a son, in fact—
and I don't want to see you get hurt. Now, when that
Deficiency Bill comes up in the Senate tomorrow you stay
away from it. Don't say a word. Great powers are behind
it, and they'll destroy you before you can even get started.
For your own sake, Jeff, and for the sake of my friendship
with your father, please, don't say a word.

Monologue Two

JEFFERSON
(reading)

"—We hold these truths to be self-evident, that all men
are created equal, that they are endowed by their Creator
with certain Unalienable Rights—that among these are Life,
Liberty and the Pursuit of Happiness. That to secure these
rights, Governments are instituted among Men, deriving
their just powers from the consent of the governed, that
whenever any form of government becomes destructive of

these ends, it is the right of the People to alter or to abolish
it, and to institute new government, laying its foundation
on such principles and organizing its powers in such form,
as to them shall seem most likely to effect their Safety and
Happiness—" Now, that's pretty swell, isn't it? I always
get such a kick outa those parts of the Declaration—especially when I can read 'em out loud to somebody.

(waving the book)

You see, that's what I had in mind about camp—except
those men said it a little better than I can. Now, you're not
gonna have a country that makes these kind of rules *work*,
if you haven't got men who've learned to tell human rights
from a punch in the nose. And funny thing about men—
they start life being boys. That's why it seemed like a pretty
good idea to take kids out of crowded cities and stuffy
basements for a few months a year—and build their bodies
and minds for a man-sized job. Those boys'll be sitting at
these desks some day. Yes—it seemed a pretty good idea—
boys coming together—all nationalities and ways of living—finding out what makes different people tick the way
they do. 'Cause I wouldn't give you a red cent for *all* your
fine rules, without there was some plain everyday, common
kindness under 'em—and a little looking-out for the next
fella. Yes—pretty important, all that. Just happens to be
blood and bone and sinew of this democracy that some great
man handed down to the human race—! That's all! But, of
course, if you need to build a dam where a camp like that
ought to be—to make some graft and pay off your political
army or something—why, that's different!

(suddenly—with strength)

No sir! If anybody here thinks I'm going back to those boys
and say to 'em: "Forget it, fellas. Everything I've told you
about the land you live in is a lotta hooey. It isn't your
country—it belongs to the James Taylors—!" No, sir, anybody that thinks that has got another think coming!

*(He breaks off, and starts a different tune,
apologetically.)*
I—I'm sorry to be coming back to that and—I'm sorry
I have to stand here—it's pretty disrespectful to this
honorable body. When I think—this was where Clay
and Calhoun and Webster spoke—Webster stood right
here by this desk—why, nobody like me ought to get in
here, in the first place—an' I hate to go on trying your
patience like this—but—well, I'm either dead right or I'm
crazy!

Knute Rockne, All American

Warner Brothers (Produced by Robert Fellows), 1940
Screenplay by Robert Buckner
Directed by Lloyd Bacon

Time: 1920s
Place: Locker room, West Point
Knute Rockne, a legendary football coach at Notre Dame,
is in the twilight of his career. In earlier days at Notre
Dame he had found a great young player, George Gipp,
who was nonchalant, thoughtful, poised—*heroic.* Rockne
and Gipp developed a quiet mutual respect. Notre Dame
was triumphant with "the Gipper" on the team. But, "the
Gipper" died suddenly, devastating Knute.

Knute commits himself even more fully to the game of
football as a sport and as a character-builder. He has stu-
pendous success. For three straight years Notre Dame is
undefeated.

Then they take on archrival Army. It's the "big game,"
but they lose. It's a personal defeat for Knute. Notre Dame

wins the next game, but Knute collapses on the field and
is hospitalized.

He is sick and confined to a hospital bed when Notre
Dame meets Army again. Rockne sneaks out of the hospital,
travels to West Point, and finds his team losing and de-
moralized. He enters the locker room at halftime and speaks
to the players.

————

*(His dark-circled eyes range over the players
for a full moment of unbroken silence.
Then quietly, as if the game didn't matter
to him)*
ROCKNE
I haven't a thing to say, boys . . . You've played a great
game . . .
(he tries to smile)
I guess we can't win 'em all.
*(He pauses, then slowly turns his wheelchair
toward the door. As he does this, he looks
straight into the face of a boy seated nearby,
and CAMERA INCLUDES HIM. The boy's
wretchedly unhappy face is typical of all the
others—boys whose hearts are wrenched
within them because they feel that they are
"letting Rockne down." Greatly moved by the
boy's look, Knute stares beyond him, as if
looking back through the years—as if
reminded of another boy's face. Slowly he
turns his wheelchair to face the crowded
room.)*
(quietly)
Boys—I'm going to tell you something I've kept to myself
for years—

(All eyes are upon Knute as he pauses, curious
at an unfamiliar ring in his voice.)
None of you ever knew George Gipp. He was long before
your time. But you know what his tradition stands for at
Notre Dame . . .
(There is a gentle, faraway look in his eyes as
he recalls the boy's words.)
Well, the last thing he said to me was—"Rock—sometime,
when the team is up against it—when things are wrong
and the breaks are beating the boys—tell them to go in
there with all they've got and win just one for the Gipper . . .
(Knute's eyes become misty and his voice is
unsteady as he finishes.)
I don't know where I'll be then, Rock," he said—"but I'll
know about it—and I'll be happy."

The Grapes of Wrath

Twentieth Century-Fox (Produced by Nunnally Johnson),
1940
Screenplay by Nunnally Johnson
Based on the novel by John Steinbeck
Directed by John Ford

Time: The Depression
Place: California Migrant Camp
Tom Joad's sharecropper family travels from the Dust Bowl
to California in search of work. Their Oklahoma farm, rav-
aged by drought, has been repossessed by the government.
Just before the journey, Tom was released from prison after
serving a four-year sentence—they said he killed a man.

Tom and his family look for work as migrant workers and are temporarily living in a work camp. Tom meets Casey, a labor activist and visionary, and witnesses his violent death at the hands of the local union busters. At the camp Tom gets caught up in a fight with camp officials, and in the melee an official is inadvertently killed. Now Tom is on the run. With the authorities after him, Tom sneaks back into the camp one night where his family is still staying to say good-bye to his Ma.

(TOM leads MA to the bench and sits her down. He sits beside her.)

They was some cops here, Ma. They was takin' down the license numbers. It looks like somebody knows sump'n. I'd like to stay. I'd like to be with ya—
(smiling)
—an' see your face when you an' Pa get settled in a nice little place. I sure wish I could see you then. But—
(shaking his head)
—I guess I won't never be able to do that. Not now.
(thoughtfully)
You know what I been thinkin' about, Ma? About Casey. About what he said, what he done, an' about how he died. An' I remember all of it. I been thinkin' about us, too— about our people livin' like pigs, an' good rich lan' layin' fallow, or maybe one fella with a million acres, while a hundred thousan' farmers is starvin'. An' I been wonderin' if all our folks got together an' yelled— They gonna drive me anyways. Soon or later they'll get me, for one thing if not another. Until then . . . But as long as I'm a outlaw, anyways, maybe I can do sump'n. Maybe I can jus' fin' out sump'n. Jus' scrounge aroun' an' try to fin' out what it is that's wrong, an' then see if they ain't sump'n could be done about it.

(worriedly)

But I ain't thought it out clear, Ma. I can't. I don't know enough.

(laughing uneasily)

Well, maybe it's like Casey says, a fella ain't got a soul of his own, but on'y a piece of a soul—the one big soul that belongs to ever'body—an then . . . Then it don't matter. There I'll be all aroun' in the dark. I'll be everywhere—wherever you look. Whenever there's a fight so hungry people can eat . . . I'll be there. Wherever there's a guy beatin' up a guy, I'll be there. I'll be in the way guys yell when they're mad an' I'll be in the way kids laugh when they're hungry an' they know supper's ready. An' when our people eat the stuff they raise, an' live in the houses they build, why, I'll be there too.

(drily, rising)

It's just stuff I been thinkin' about. Give me your han', Ma. Good-bye.

The Westerner

Produced by Samuel Goldwyn, 1940
Screenplay by Jo Swerling and Niven Busch
Based on a story by Stuart N. Lake
Directed by William Wyler

Time: 1843
Place: Vinagaroon, Texas, West of Pecos
In the Wild West town of Vinagaroon, Judge Roy Bean presides over a somewhat unorthodox court. His trials take place in the local saloon, his jury is comprised of the saloon's patrons, and he brings his court to order not with a gavel but with a gun.

One day, a cowboy, Cole Hardin, is brought into court by some men who accuse him of horse stealing. Bean informs Hardin that horse stealing is a capital offense, and therefore he must pay the consequences.

While the jury is deliberating Hardin notices a large picture of Lillie Langtry over the judge's bar. He mentions to the judge that he knows Lillie, and Bean eagerly tries to get Hardin to tell him about her. Hardin stalls a little to tease the judge and get him more excited. Finally he begins to describe Lillie to the judge, who is now leaning dreamy-eyed on the bar.

———

COLE
(describing LILLIE LANGTRY to JUDGE ROY BEAN)

Ever been down around Lanno Bay? Well, you know how it is just before the sun sets? You can look out and that water ain't exactly blue and it ain't exactly purple—it's a sort of a color a man can feel but he can't put a name to? Well, that's Lillie's eyes. Her hair . . . that's a tough one, Judge. You know how bright and coppery and gold-like a young chestnut horse is—running in the bright sun? Well, her hair looks something like that in the daytime. But, you know at dusk, when you look off and a prairie fire's reflected in the sky—a sort of deep, lovely kind of blushing red? Well, that'll give you a rough idea. I've got a lock of her hair. But I wouldn't part with that lock of hair for anything in the world.

The Lady Eve

Paramount Pictures (Produced by Paul Jones), 1941
Screenplay by Preston Sturges
Directed by Preston Sturges

Time: 1941
Place: On board a luxury ship bound from South America
to the U.S.A.
Traveling con artists, disguised as elegant passengers, have
found their way on board a luxury liner. They are Jean
Harrington, Jean's father (the "Colonel"), and her father's
sidekick, Muggsy. Also on board is Charles Pike, a wealthy,
handsome explorer/scientist on his way home from adven-
tures in the jungles of the Amazon. Pike is being pursued
by all the eligible young ladies on the ship but is shy and
eludes capture.

Eating alone one evening in the ship's sumptuous dining
room, Pike is repeatedly approached by one young woman
after another—some subtle, others not. Jean, seated at a
nearby table with her father and Muggsy, surreptitiously
observes Pike and his pursuers by using her compact mirror. Her monologue is a running commentary on the com-
ical scene at Pike's table.

JEAN
(looking into her mirror)
Not good enough. I said they're not good enough for him.
Every Jane in the room is giving him the thermometer and
he feels they're just a waste of time. He's returning to his
book . . . he's deeply immersed in it . . . He sees no one
except watch his head turn when that kid goes by . . . it
won't do you any good, dear, he's a bookworm, but swing

them anyway . . . yes, they're straight . . . you don't have
to worry, but she's a little flat in the front . . . now here
comes one that's a little flat behind . . . that's right, dear,
just a quick one then back to the book. The dropped 'ker-
chief! That hasn't been used since Lillie Langtry . . . you'll
have to pick it up yourself, madam . . . it's a shame, but
he doesn't care for the flesh; he'll never see it. That's
right . . . pick it up . . . it was worth trying anyway, wasn't
it? . . . Look at the girl over to his left . . . look over to
your left, bookworm . . . there's a girl pining for you . . . a
little further . . . just a little further. THERE! Now wasn't
that worth looking for? See those nice store teeth, all beam-
ing at you. Why, she recognizes you! She's up . . . she's
down, she can't make up her mind, she's up again! She
recognizes you! She's coming over to speak to you. The
suspense is killing me. "Why, for heaven's sake, aren't you
Fuzzy Oathammer I went to manual training school with
in Louisville? Oh, you're not? Well, you certainly look
exactly like him . . . it's certainly a remarkable resem-
blance, but if you're not going to ask me to sit down I
suppose you're not going to ask me to sit down . . . I'm
very sorry. I certainly hope I haven't caused you any em-
barrassment, you so-and-so," so here she goes back to the
table. Imagine thinking she could get away with anything
like that with me . . . I wonder if my tie's on straight . . .
I certainly upset them, don't I? Now who else is after me?
Ah! The lady champion wrestler, wouldn't she make an
armful . . . Oh, you don't like her either . . . Well, what
are you going to do about it . . . Oh, you just can't stand
it any more . . . you're leaving . . . these women just don't
give you a moment's peace, do they . . . Well, go ahead!
Go sulk in your cabin! Go soak your head and see if I care.

Meet John Doe

Liberty Films (Produced by Frank Capra), 1941
Screenplay by Robert Riskin
Directed by Frank Capra

Time: 1941

Place: A city in the Midwest, U.S.A.

Ann Mitchell, a reporter in her twenties, works at a Mid-western newspaper that has just been taken over by new management. Her editor, Hank Connell, informs her that the new owner, D. B. Norton, is axing her column because it's all "lavender and old lace" and not in sync with the paper's new format.

In a last-gasp effort to keep her column, Ann concocts a letter written by one "John Doe" stating that "four years ago I was fired from my job . . . I can't get another . . . slimy politics create unemployment and in protest I'm going to jump off the roof of City Hall." The letter creates public outrage and succeeds in getting the massive audience the owner wants. The bigwigs at the newspaper are pleased, and Ann gets to keep her column. But when Connell finds out Ann faked the letter, he's angry and wants the paper to drop the entire business.

He suggests that the paper report that its staff convinced John Doe to change his mind and therefore has saved his life. Ann vehemently disagrees with Connell and tells him so.

ANN

Wait a minute! Listen you great big wonderful genius of a newspaperman! You came down here to shoot some life into this dying paper, didn't you? Well, the whole town's curious about John Doe, and boom, just like that you're going to bury him. There's enough circulation in that man to create a shortage in the ink market! Now, look, suppose there was a John Doe—and he walked into this office. What would you do? Find him a job and forget the whole business? Not me! I'd make a deal with him! When you get hold of a stunt that sells papers you don't drop it like a hot potato! Why, this is good for at least a couple of months. You know what I'd do? Between now and say Christmas, when he's gonna jump, I'd run a daily yarn starting with his boyhood, his schooling, his first job! A wide-eyed youngster facing a chaotic world. The problem of the average man, of all the John Doe's in the world. Now, then comes the drama. He meets discouragement. He finds the world has feet of clay. His ideals crumble, so what does he do? He decides to commit suicide in protest against the state of civilization. He thinks of the river! But no, no, he has a better idea. The City Hall. Why? Because he wants to attract attention. He wants to get a few things off his chest, and that's the only way he can get himself heard. So! So he writes me a letter and I dig him up. He pours out his story to me, and from now on we quote: "I protest," by John Doe. He protests against all the evils in the world, the greed, the lust, the hate, the fear, all of man's inhumanity to man. Arguments will start. Should he commit suicide or should he not? People will write in pleading with him. But no! No, Sir! John Doe will remain adamant! On Christmas Eve, hot or cold, he goes! See?

Hail the Conquering Hero

Paramount Pictures (Produced by Preston Sturges), 1944
Screenplay by Preston Sturges
Directed by Preston Sturges

Time: 1944
Place: Oakridge, California
Woodrow Truesmith, in his early twenties, is the son of a much decorated Marine Corps hero who died in World War I. He was raised revering the Marines. He knows every battle and skirmish in Marine Corps history, and when America enters World War II, he tries to enlist.

Because of severe hay fever, Woodrow is given a medical discharge and has to find work in a shipyard instead. He is ashamed to tell his mother, so he writes her letters as if he were at the front in the South Pacific. He has someone mail the letters from "over there."

When the war ends, Woodrow heads home. On the way he stops at a bar and encounters a group of Marines home from the fighting in Guadalcanal.

By coincidence, one of the Marines fought under Woodrow's father in the World War I. Out of respect for Woodrow's father, and sympathy for Woodrow's dilemma, the Marines decide to accompany him home as a war "hero" — fitted with a borrowed uniform replete with medals and ribbons.

Woodrow resists, but he cannot stop what has already been set in motion. Not only is he given a hero's welcome by the town, but he's also elected mayor. Finally he *must* end the deception. He speaks to a crowd of townspeople.

WOODROW

I came here this morning to say goodbye to you . . . to tell you that I had been called back into the Marine Corps for limited service . . . and that for that reason I would be unable to run for Mayor. Well, I'm not going to do it! You'd better save your hoorays for somebody else—for somebody else who deserves them—like Doc Bissell here, who's tried for so long to serve you, only you didn't know a good man when you saw one, so you always elected a phoney instead . . . until a bigger phoney came along—then you naturally wanted him. This should have been the happiest day of my life. It could have been. Instead, it's the bitterest. It says in the Bible: "My cup runneth over." Well, my cup runneth over—with gall. This is the last act; the farce is over; the lying is finished—and the coward is at last cured of his fears. I was born in this town. My father was born here. Most of this town is on my grandfather's homestead. My grandfather was an honorable man. So was my father. I've sold papers on the street to most of you who are here this morning. I've known you all my life. Your affection means a great deal to me and now that I've lost the chance forever I—I want you all to know how much it would have meant to me to be the Mayor, or the City Clerk, or the Assistant City Clerk or the dogcatcher of this town which was my grandfather's farm. By the same token, I would have gladly given my life to have earned just one of the many ribbons you've seen on these brave men's chests. If I could only reach as high as my father's shoestrings my whole life would be justified and I would stand before you proudly, instead of the thief and coward that I am. I say a coward because I postponed until now what I should have told you a year ago when I was discharged from the Marine Corps for medical unfitness . . . a coward because I didn't want my mother to know. Well, it wasn't to save her—it was to save me. A thief—because I stole your admiration. . . . I stole the ribbons I wore—I stole this nomination. I have never been in Guadal— I have never been in

Guadalcanal or any place else. I've been working in a shipyard for the last year. I've never received medals of any
description—naturally since I've never fought— Uh, two
days ago I—I—decided to come home and since I'd wrote
to my mother that I was overseas—I—I—had to have some
ribbons so I—I bought some in a hock shop. When I was
all dressed up I—I—met some real Marines and I fooled
them just as much as I did the rest of you . . . not that I
really wanted to fool any of you— I—I—just wanted to
come home. I've told you this because too many men have
bled and died for you and for me to live this lie any longer.
I guess that's why I told you. I certainly didn't mean to
when I came in—I'm going home now to pack my things
so this will probably be my last chance to say goodbye to
you. I know my mother will give you back the mortgage
and I hope you won't hold it against her that her son didn't
quite come through. There's no use telling you I'm sorry—
because I wish I was dead. I—uh—that's all.

It's a Wonderful Life

RKO/Liberty Films (Produced by Frank Capra), 1946
Screenplay by Frances Goodrich, Albert Hackett,
and Frank Capra
Directed by Frank Capra

Time: 1930s
Place: Bedford Falls, a small New England town
It's a Wonderful Life is the story of George Bailey, who,
in a moment of crisis, wishes he'd never been born and
decides to kill himself. Just as George is on the brink of
suicide, Clarence, his guardian angel, is dispatched from
heaven to rescue him. He shows George what life would

have been like in Bedford Falls if, in fact, he hadn't been born. In so doing, he proves to George how valuable his life has been and how he's enriched the lives of everyone with whom he came in contact.

In a series of flashbacks we see episodes of George's life starting from boyhood. In one of these George is about to embark on a trip to Europe and then go off to college. His plans are upended, however, when his father, Peter Bailey, has a sudden stroke and dies. George must cancel his trip to Europe and spend the next few months straightening things out at his father's company, Bailey Brothers Building and Loan.

The day that George is finally to leave for college, there's a meeting of the board of the Building and Loan to appoint a successor to Peter Bailey. As George is about to leave the meeting and hop into a taxi, Old Man Potter, the richest, meanest, and most powerful man in town, announces to the other board members that he doesn't think the Building and Loan is necessary to the town. He makes a motion to dissolve the institution. He accuses Peter Bailey of having been a poor businessman with so-called high ideals. George responds to Old Man Potter.

———

GEORGE

Just a minute—just a minute. Now, hold on, Mr. Potter. You're *right* when you say my father was no *business* man. I know that. Why he ever started this cheap, penny-ante Building and Loan, I'll *never* know. But neither you nor anybody else can say anything against his character, because his whole life was . . . Why, in the twenty-five years since he and Uncle Billy started this thing, he never once thought of himself. Isn't that right, Uncle Billy? He didn't save enough money to send *Harry* to school, let alone me. But he *did* help a few people get out of your slums, Mr.

Potter. And what's wrong with that? Why . . . here, you're all businessmen here. Doesn't it make them better citizens? Doesn't it make them better customers? You . . . you said . . . What'd you say just a minute ago? . . . They had to wait and save their money before they even ought to think of a decent home. Wait! Wait for what? Until their children grow up and leave them? Until they're so old and broken-down that they . . . Do you know how long it takes a working man to save five thousand dollars? Just remember this, Mr. Potter, that this rabble you're talking about . . . they do most of the working and paying and living and dying in this community. Well, is it too much to have them work and pay and live and die in a couple of decent rooms and a bath? Anyway, my *father* didn't think so. People were human beings to him, but to you, a warped, frustrated old man, they're cattle. Well, in my book he died a much richer man than you'll ever be!

[POTTER

I'm not interested in your book. I'm talking about the Building and Loan.]

GEORGE

I know very well what you're talking about. You're talking about something you can't get your fingers on, and it's galling you. That's what you're talking about, I know.

(to the Board)

Well, I've said too much. I . . . You're the Board here. You do what you want with this thing. Just one thing more, though. This town needs this mealy one-horse institution if only to have some place where people can come without crawling to Potter. Come on, Uncle Billy!

The Treasure of the Sierra Madre

Warner Brothers (Produced by Henry Blanke), 1948
Screenplay by John Huston
Based on the novel by B. Traven
Directed by John Huston

Time: 1948
Place: Mexico
Two drifters join forces with Howard, a down-and-out old prospector, to search for gold in the Mexican hills. They ask him if there really is gold to be found. Howard responds.

HOWARD
(the old man)

Gold in Mexico? Sure there is. Not ten days from here by rail and pack train, a mountain's waiting for the right guy to come along, discover her treasure, and then tickle her until she lets him have it. The question is, are you the right guy . . . ? Real bonanzas are few and far between and they take a lot of finding. Answer me this one, will you? Why's gold worth some twenty bucks per ounce? A thousand men, say, go searching for gold. After six months one of 'em is lucky—one out of the ten thousand. His find represents not only his own labor but that of the nine hundred ninety-nine others to boot. Six thousand months or fifty years of scrabbling over mountains, going hungry and thirsty. An ounce of gold, mister, is worth what it is because of the human labor that went into the finding and the getting of it. There's no other explanation, mister. In itself, gold ain't good for anything much except to make jewelry and gold teeth. Gold's a devilish sort of thing anyway.

(He has a faraway look in his eye.)

When you go out you tell yourself, "I'll be satisfied with

twenty-five thousand handsome smackers worth of it, so help me Lord and cross my heart." Fine resolution. After months of sweating yourself dizzy and growing short on provisions and finding nothing, you come down to twenty thousand and then fifteen, until finally you say, "Lord, let me find just five thousand dollars' worth and I'll never ask anything more of you the rest of my life." Here in the Oso Negro it seems like a lot. But I tell you, if you were to make a real find, you couldn't be dragged away. Not even the threat of miserable death would stop you from trying to add ten thousand more. And when you'd reach twenty-five, you'd want to make it fifty, and at fifty, a hundred— and so on. Like at roulette . . . just one more turn . . . always one more. You lose your sense of values and your character changes entirely. Your soul stops being the same as it was before. I've dug in Alaska, and in Canada and Colorado. I was in the crowd in British Honduras where I made my boat fare back home and almost enough over to cure me of a fever I'd caught. I've dug in California and Australia . . . all over this world practically, and I know what gold does to men's souls.

Adam's Rib

MGM (Produced by Lawrence Weingarten), 1949
Screenplay by Ruth Gordon and Garson Kanin
Directed by George Cukor

Time: 1949
Place: Manhattan
Adam and Amanda Bonner are happily married. They are both attorneys. He is a prosecutor, and she is a prominent defense lawyer.

As courtroom rivals, they revel in matching wits and legal skills. This trial, however, is different. The issues raised, and the legal battle waged, set their relationship—both professional and personal—comically on its ear.

Doris Attinger is on trial for the attempted murder of her husband, Warren. She has shot and wounded him after following him to the apartment of another woman, Beryl Caighn.

Amanda is convinced that there's a double standard—that if Doris were a man, the jury would acquit her, finding her assault justifiable. Society excuses jealous behavior in a man, Amanda stresses, but a woman driven to drastic action is rarely understood and is immediately and unequivocally censured.

Adam prefers to see it as a more cut-and-dried case of premeditated murder.

The following monologues are Adam's and Amanda's summations to the jury. (Note: When Adam refers to the "tenderly trimmed bonnet" worn by the defendant and says he paid for it, it is because he knows Amanda bought the bonnet with money from *their* checking account.)

Monologue One

(The crowded courtroom. Up and down the sides of the room, rows of people standing. The press table is busy. AMANDA, on her feet, has reached the climax of her peroration.)

AMANDA
(to the JURORS)

—and so the question here is equality before the law—regardless of religion, color, wealth—or as in this instance—sex. Excuse me.

(She removes her jacket and takes a sip of

water. Now, in blouse and skirt, she returns to
the fray.)

Law, like man, is composed of two parts. Just as a man is
body and soul, so is the law letter and spirit. The law says,
"Thou shalt not kill!" Yet men *have* killed and proved a
reason and been set free. Self-defense—defense of others,
of wife or children or home. If a thief breaks into your home
and you shoot him, the law will not deal harshly with you.
Nor, indeed, should it. Thus, you are asked to judge not
whether or not these acts were committed, but to what
extent they were justified. Now, Ladies and Gentlemen of
the Jury, I respectfully request that you join me in a re-
vealing experiment. I ask you all to direct your attention
to the defendant, Mrs. Attinger. Now, keep looking at her.
Keep watching. Listen carefully. Look at her. Look at her
hard.

(hypnotically)

Now imagine her a man. Go on now. Use your imagination.
Think of her as a man sitting there. Think of her as a man
sitting there, accused of a like crime. Think! All right, that's
enough. Now, continuing, I ask you to hold that impression.
And look at *Mr.* Attinger. And suppose him a woman. Try.
Try hard. All right, thank you. And now, Miss Caighn.
She's the third party. She's that slick homewrecker. Picture
her so. A wolf. You know the type. All right. Now you have
it. Judge it so. An unwritten law stands back of a man who
fights to defend his home. Apply the same to this maltreated
wife and neglected mother. We ask you no more. Equality!

Monologue Two

ADAM
(good and rattled)

The purpose of a summation, as I have said, or rather as I

meant to say, *is*, as I understand it, no more or less than—
if in a Lourt of Caw, Court of Law—
> *(he is hopelessly muddled and bogged down*
> *now)*

Excuse me, ladies and gentlemen.
> *(He takes a drink, glares at AMANDA, who*
> *smiles back her sweetest smile.)*

Let me begin again. As a jury, you are a most fortunate
body. Your decision here is simple and clear. You need
only decide whether she fired her husband at the, pistol
at her husband, and at Beryl Caighn. She has told you that
she did. What, then, is there left for you to decide? Whether
or not she was attempting to kill her husband, Miss Caighn,
or both. I smile. I find it difficult to proceed without burst-
ing into laughter at the childish pimslicity of the answer.
And at the puny excuse, well after the fact, that—
> *(his voice drips with sarcasm)*

—she only meant to frighten them. Simplicity! This being
the case, why not blank cartridges? Why not a cap pistol?
Why any pistol at all? Why not simply appearing? That
would have been frightening enough. Wouldn't it? As a
citizen—a law-abiding citizen—I resent any neighbor who
dares to take the law into her own hands—to create an
individual interpretation for herself alone. Now as to the
character of this Doris Attinger. I'm afraid we know little
about it—or about Doris Attinger. We have not seen Doris
Attinger here. What we have seen has been a performance
complete with costume and makeup. Carefully coached by
her artful counsel, she has presented a gentle facade. A
sweet face, crowned by a tenderly trimmed little bonnet.
I found it difficult to be taken in, ladies and gentlemen,
since *I* am the one who paid for the bonnet!
> *(He draws a slip from his pocket and shows it*
> *to the jury.)*

And here is my receipt to prove it!
> *(He hands it to AMANDA.)*

Any objection to my showing it to the Court and to the Jury?

A Letter to Three Wives

Twentieth Century-Fox (Produced by Sol C. Siegel), 1949
Screenplay by Joseph L. Mankiewicz
Directed by Joseph L. Mankiewicz

Time: 1948
Place: Upper-middle-class suburb, U.S.A.

Three young suburban wives in their twenties, fellow country club members and friends, receive a letter from another woman from the area whom they all know slightly, saying that she has run off with one of their husbands—*which* husband, she doesn't say.

The three are left to wonder, all day, whose marriage is over. The trauma of this event sets off a flurry of self-examination and personal revelation among the three women and, eventually, between the husbands and their wives.

One of the wives is Deborah Bishop, who met her husband during the war—she was a Wave, he a sailor. The other women are Rita Phipps, a writer of material for radio shows; and Lora Mae Hollingsway, a tough cookie who looked for a rich husband and found him. Deborah speaks to the two other wives.

DEBORAH
(abruptly)

I think I've got a sick headache and can't go. Because.

Because—I'm wrong. Wrong—how? How wrong? Every
which way. For Brad. For his friends—you, your husband
and the rest I haven't met yet, the country club, the town . . .
I'm scared. I'm so scared, I'm sick.

(turns away, moves a drunken step or two)

Too many Martinis, right . . . ? More tonight, right here
getting dressed—dressed, ha ha—than the whole rest of
my life . . . tonight. Worse, even, than my first night in
the Waves. I'd never been away from home before—but
we were *all* in the same spot, everything happening to *all*
of us for the first time. Here . . . I'm the only—new girl.

(slowly turns back to face RITA)

Ever read in the picture magazines about Farmer So-and-
So and his model farm, kitchen and life? Well—it wasn't
us or anybody we knew. . . . Pappa'd just get the thresher
paid up in time to start paying on the new separator . . . till
I was thirteen a bus took me three miles that way to gram-
mar school, and till I was seventeen another bus took me
eleven miles *that* way to high school, and after that I stayed
home until one day I took a bus fifty-eight miles *that* way
to join the Navy—

(pause)

—and see and free the world and meet Bradbury Bishop.
And fall in love. And marry Bradbury Bishop. Why not?

(another pause)

Why not, I said to myself . . . I was quite a girl in the
Navy, the head of my class, hooray for me—and pretty cute
in that uniform . . . that uniform. It's the great level-leler—

(she has a little trouble with the word)

—you couldn't tell me from Vassar or Smith or Long Island . . . I was the girl downstairs, in the picture on the
table. But that isn't me. This is me.

(then in sudden emotion)

What do you people talk about? Years of growing up together, thousands of first names and private memories, how

do I fit in? Running a house, making friends, filling the day—Mrs. Bradbury Bishop—what's she like? Fun to be with, smart as a whip, pretty, too, no wonder Brad Bishop married her, the lucky stiff—Rita, look at me! Look at my mail-order dress that's four years old and awful even then! Oh, what am I going to do?

All the King's Men

Columbia Pictures (Produced by Robert Rossen), 1949
Screenplay by Robert Rossen
Based on the novel by Robert Penn Warren
Directed by Robert Rossen

Time: 1949
Place: Deep South
Based on the life of the populist politician Huey Long of Louisiana, *All the King's Men* looks at the rise and fall of Willie Stark. Willie begins as an idealistic young back-country boy in a small Southern town. An outspoken activist, Willie becomes a lawyer to help the people rise up in the fight against political corruption.

With the support of the working people Willie eventually sweeps to power himself. But he ends up using, and being used by, the rich, powerful, and corrupt. In his efforts to create an effective political machine geared toward preserving his power base and position, Willie turns his back on the people who elected him.

This monologue occurs during Willie's initial rise to power. Stark has arrived at the Upton Fairgrounds at a big country barbecue to speak to the crowds. He's running for governor for the first time. Willie's been drinking and cannot focus on the written speech in his hands, so he focuses on the faces in the crowd. Throwing his prepared speech away, Willie begins.

WILLIE

My friends . . .

(He turns his face from side to side, and fumbles in the right side of his coat pocket to fish out his speech.)

My friends . . . I . . .

(He tries to focus on the speech, which he clutches before his eyes with both hands. Then he lifts his head, and looks directly at the people who have come to hear him. As he speaks, the camera focuses on the faces of these people: the farmers, workers, hicks, rednecks who are WILLIE's audience, WILLIE's people.)

I have a speech here. It's a speech about what this state needs. There's no need in my telling you what this state needs. You are the state and you know what you need . . . You over there . . . look at your pants. Have they got holes in the knees? Listen to your stomach. Did you ever hear it rumble from hunger? . . . And you, what about your crops? Did they ever rot in the field because the road was so bad you couldn't get them to market? . . . And you. What about your kids? Are they growing up ignorant as dirt, ignorant as you, 'cause there's no school for them? . . . No, I'm not going to read you any speech.

(He throws his speech away. DUFFY looks alarmed.)

But I am going to tell you a story. It's a funny story . . . So get ready to laugh. Get ready to bust your sides laughing, 'cause it's sure a funny story. It's about a hick . . . a hick like you, if you please. Yeah, like you. He grew up on the

dirt roads and gully washes of a farm. He knew what it was
to get up before dawn and get feed and slop and milk before
breakfast . . . and then set out before sunup and walk six
miles to a one-room, slab-sided schoolhouse. Oh, this hick
knew what it was to be a hick, all right. He figured if he
was going to get anything done, he had to do it himself.
So he sat up nights and studied books. He studied law
because he thought he might be able to change things
some . . . for himself, and for folks like him.

*(SUGAR BOY listens intently, sharing in the
anger in WILLIE's speech.)*

No, I'm not going to lie to you. He didn't start off thinking
about the hicks and all the wonderful things he was going
to do for them. No. No, he started off thinking of number
one. But something came to him on the way. How he could
do nothing for himself without the help of the people. That's
what came to him. And it also came to him, with the powerful force of God's own lightning, back in his home country, when a schoolhouse collapsed because it was built of
politics . . . rotten brick. It killed and mangled a dozen
kids. But you know that story. The people were his friends
because he fought that rotten brick. And some of the politicians down in the city, they knew that . . . So they rode
up to his house in a big, fine, shiny car and said as how
they wanted him to run for governor . . .

*(DUFFY fidgets as WILLIE continues to pace
and speak, his face filled with conviction, and
with fury.)*

So they told the hick . . . and he swallowed it. He looked
in his heart and he thought in all humility how he'd like to
try and change things. He was just a country boy who
thought that even the plainest, poorest man can be governor if his fellow citizens find he's got the stuff for the job.
Well, those fellows in the striped pants . . . they saw the
hick and they took him in.

(He points his finger at DUFFY, who is coming over to speak to him.)

[DUFFY

(low voice)

Willie, what are you trying to do?]

(WILLIE turns on him, roaring.)

WILLIE

There he is! There's your Judas Iscariot.

(He pushes DUFFY across the platform.)

Look at him . . . lickspittle . . . nose-wiper.

(DUFFY gestures frantically to the band.)

[DUFFY

Play! Play!]

WILLIE

(pushing him again)

Look at him!

[DUFFY

Play anything.]

(The band starts to play, adding to the pandemonium. WILLIE shouts above it.)

WILLIE

Look at him! Joe Harrison's dummy! Look at him!

[DUFFY

That's a lie!]

WILLIE

Look at him!

(DUFFY signals to some of his goons standing near the platform.)

[DUFFY

Go get him, boys . . . go get him.]

(SUGAR BOY leaps up on the platform, his pistol drawn and pointed at DUFFY's men. WILLIE throws up his arms to silence the crowd.)

WILLIE

Now, shut up! Shut up, all of you. Now, listen to me, you
hicks. Yeah, you're hicks too, and they fooled you a thousand times, just like they fooled me. But this time I'm going
to fool somebody. I'm going to stay in this race. I'm on my
own and I'm out for blood.

(*The camera moves in close on WILLIE's face.*)
Listen to me, you hicks . . .

The African Queen

IFD/Romulus-Horizon (Produced by Sam Spiegel), 1951
Screenplay by James Agee
Based on the novel by C. S. Forester
Directed by John Huston

Time: World War I
Place: Central Africa
Charlie Allnutt is a rough-edged Cockney Englishman approaching middle age. He runs the *African Queen*, a de-
crepit but effective mail and supply boat—a lifeline for the
colonial settlements and missions upriver in Central Africa
during World War I.

Brother Sayer and his spinster sister, Rose, oversee these
missions in the jungle. Products of the British upper class,
they silently endure Charlie's libertine drinking, smoking,
and crude humor.

As the war approaches, German troops send a commando
squad to sack and burn the Sayers' settlement. Rose's brother
dies, and Charlie, who happens on the smoldering ruins,
offers to take Rose out of danger on the *African Queen* with
him.

As the journey begins, the two suffer each other's company. Charlie drinks gin, smokes, and rarely bathes. Rose "takes tea" on the oily rag-strewn deck of the boat, trying to maintain propriety and dignity. But eventually the barriers between them break down as they face the dangers of the river and the Germans.

This monologue occurs when Rose and Charlie are still at an impasse. Charlie tries his best to gain her favor and break her chilly silence.

ALLNUTT
(brightly)
Well, Miss, 'ere we are, everything ship-shape, like they say. Great thing to 'ave a lyedy aboard, with clean 'abits. Sets me a good example. A man alone, 'e gets to livin' like a bloomin' 'og.
(no answer)
Then, too, with me, it's always—put things orf. Never do todye wot ya can put orf till tomorrer.
(He chuckles and looks at her, expecting her to smile. Not a glimmer from ROSE.)
But you: business afore pleasure, every time. Do yer pers'nal laundry, make yerself spic an' span, get all the mendin' out o' the way, an' *then*, an' *hone-ly then*, set down to a nice quiet hour with the *Good*-Book.
(He watches for something; she registers nothing.)
I tell you, it's a model for me, like. An inspiration. I ain't got that ole engine so clean in years; inside an' out, Miss. Just look at 'er, Miss! She practically sparkles.
(ROSE evidently does not hear him.)
Myself, too. Guess you ain't never 'ad a look at me without whiskers an' all cleaned up, 'ave you, Miss?

(no look)

Freshens you up, too; if I only 'ad clean clothes, like you.
Now you: why you could be at 'igh tea.

(no recognition from ROSE)

'Ow *'bout* some tea, Miss, come to think of it? Don't you
stir; I'll get it ready.

(a little silence)

'Ow's the book, Miss?

(no answer)

Not that I ain't read it, some—that is to say, me ole lyedy
read me stories out of it.

(no answer; pause)

'Ow 'bout readin' it out loud, eh, Miss?

(silence)

I'd like to 'ave a little spiritual comfort m'self.

(silence; flaring up)

An' you call yerself a Christian!

(silence)

You 'ear me, Miss.

(silence)

Don't yer?

*(silence; a bright cruel idea; louder, leaning to
her)*

Don't yer?

(silence; suddenly at the top of his lungs)

HUH??

The Day the Earth Stood Still

Twentieth Century-Fox (Produced by Julian Blaustein), 1951
Screenplay by Edmund H. North
Directed by Robert Wise

Time: 1951
Place: Washington, D.C.
A spaceship lands amid the monuments of the nation's capitol.

Klaatu, an emissary from another planet, emerges from the ship. He appears human and has an aristocratic bearing and gentle grace. With him is his protector, a gigantic robot called Gort, who is indestructible and responds only to Klaatu's commands.

Klaatu has a message for the people of Earth, but representatives of the various world governments mistrust him, even though he pleads that he comes in peace. He is attacked and injured and must go into hiding. Taking on an assumed identity, he meets and observes average Earthlings and learns about the planet. With the help of a prominent physicist he attempts to convene all the Earth's leaders. But he is tracked down and killed. Gort, however, rescues Klaatu and brings him back to life.

Klaatu finally delivers his message to Earth from the steps of his departing spaceship, protected by Gort.

KLAATU
(straightforwardly, with almost stern authority)
I am leaving soon and you will forgive me if I speak bluntly.
(He pauses, studying the faces.)
The Universe grows smaller every day—and the threat of aggression by any group—anywhere—can no longer be tolerated. There must be security for *all*—or no one is

secure . . . This does not mean giving up any freedom except the freedom to act irresponsibly. Your ancestors knew this when they made laws to govern themselves—and hired policemen to enforce them. We of the other planets have long accepted this principle. We have an organization for the mutual protection of all planets—and for the complete elimination of aggression. A sort of United Nations on the Planetary level . . . The test of any such higher authority, of course, is the police force that supports it. For *our* policemen we created a race of robots—

(indicating GORT)

Their function is to patrol the planets—in space ships like this one—and preserve the peace. In matters of aggression we have given them absolute power over us. At the first sign of violence they act *automatically* against the aggressor. And the penalty for provoking their action is too terrible to risk. The result is that we live in peace, without arms or armies, secure in the knowledge that we are free from aggression and war—free to pursue more profitable enterprises.

(after a pause)

We do not pretend to have achieved perfection—but we do have a system—and it *works*.

(with straightforward candor)

I came here to give you the facts. It is no concern of ours how you run your own planet—but if you threaten to *extend* your violence, this Earth of yours will be reduced to a burned-out cinder. Your choice is simple. Join us and live in peace. Or pursue your present course—and face obliteration.

(after a pause)

We will be waiting for your answer. The decision rests with *you*.

(CAMERA MOVES along a row of their faces, stunned and silent, their minds unable to cope

with the enormity of what they have heard.
CAMERA MOVES IN on KLAATU as he is
saying goodbye to BARNHARDT and HELEN.
He turns then and speaks to GORT.)

KLAATU

Gort—veracto.

East of Eden

Warner Brothers (Produced by Elia Kazan), 1954
Screenplay by Paul Osborn
Based on the novel by John Steinbeck
Directed by Elia Kazan

Time: 1917
Place: Salinas Valley, California
Based on the John Steinbeck novel, the film chronicles the life of the Trask family—Adam Trask and his two teenaged sons, Caleb and Aron.

The dark secret of Cal and Aron's lives, hidden from them by their stern Bible-quoting father, is that their mother, thought to be long gone, runs a prosperous brothel and gaming house in a small California town not far from the Trasks' farming community.

The story is often thought of as an allusion to the biblical Cain and Abel. Cal, the "bad" brother, is impulsive and wild. Aron is engaged to Abra, a pretty local girl. He seems naive, responsible and stable but is self-sacrificing and cold. He attempts to please his father by adhering to a strict moral code. Cal wants his father's love and approval but is rebellious and independent.

Cal is desperate to prove himself to his father, but a plan he has, to increase their farm's profits during the war through new cash crops, backfires. Adam Trask is critical and dismissive, disparaging Cal as a war profiteer. He refuses the money Cal offers him from the profits of the new crops.

To unmask Aron's pose of moral superiority Cal forces Aron to discover the truth about their mother. He brings him face-to-face with her and shatters Aron's idealized fantasy.

Abra begins to lose her dutiful feelings for Aron and becomes attracted to the charismatic Cal. Abra's sweetness and strength break through Cal's defenses.

After his disillusionment at discovering his mother, Aron begins to drink. He is driven to volunteer for the war, and is killed.

Adam Trask has a stroke. He is paralyzed and cannot speak. Abra, now deeply in love with Cal, goes to Trask's bedside to speak to him about his relationship with Cal.

ABRA
(softly)

Mr. Trask.

(She waits.)

Mr. Trask—can you hear *me?* Is it just Cal you won't answer? Can you answer?

(Adam makes no sign.)

I think you can understand me, though. I think behind your eyes you're just as alert as ever and understand everything I say—only you can't show it.

(She pauses.)

Mr. Trask, it's awful not to be loved. It's the worst thing in the world. Don't ask me—even if you could—how I know that. I just know it. It makes you mean—and violent—and cruel. And that's the way Cal has always felt, Mr. Trask. All his life! Maybe you didn't mean it that way—

but it's true. You never gave him your love. You never asked for his. You never asked him for one thing.

(She pauses; Adam doesn't speak.)

Cal did something very bad and I'm not asking you to forgive him—or bless him or anything like that. Cal has got to forgive you—for not having loved him—or for not having shown your love. And he has forgiven you. I know he has. But you must give him some sign, Mr. Trask— some sign that you love him—or he'll never be a man. All his life he'll feel guilty and alone unless you release him.

(She pauses.)

I love Cal, Mr. Trask. And I want him to be happy and strong and whole. And only you can do it. Try! Please try! Find a way to show him! Ask for something. Let him help you, so he knows you love him. Let him *do* for you—

(she looks at him a moment more)

Excuse me, Mr. Trask, for daring to speak to you this way— if you hear me—but I had to!

*(Upset, she hurries out of the room to the hall
outside of Adam's room.)*

On the Waterfront

Columbia Pictures (Produced by Sam Spiegel), 1954
Screenplay by Budd Schulberg
Based on an original story by Budd Schulberg
Suggested by a series of articles by Malcolm Johnson
Directed by Elia Kazan

Time: 1954
Place: The docks of Hoboken, New Jersey
In the 1950s, the longshoremen's union is mob-controlled, wracked by graft and corruption, and sustained by a "code

of silence." A crime commission is investigating the union, but few members on the waterfront will talk. Those who *do*—the "pigeons"—wind up dead.

Terry Malloy, "a wiry, jaunty, waterfront hanger-on in his late twenties," an ex-prizefighter, is now a dockworker. He hangs out with his older brother, Charley, who works for the corrupt union boss, Johnny Friendly.

A fellow dockworker, Joey Doyle, talks to the commission, and Charley gets Terry, unwittingly, to help set Doyle up for murder. Terry was sure "the guys were only gonna work him over a little bit," but at the news of Doyle's death Terry's conscience begins to trouble him.

In the aftermath of the murder, Terry reacquaints himself and falls in love with Doyle's sister, Edie, and also makes contact with the waterfront priest, Father Barry. Father Barry is a fighter himself—for the souls of the workmen and against the injustices of the mob that rules the workers' lives.

A tough-talking, iron-willed activist, Father Barry tries to convince the men to follow their consciences, defy the union, and cooperate with the commission's investigation.

Monologue One. After Doyle, another longshoreman, Kayo Dugan, who has been cooperating with the investigation, is also killed in an "accident" on the docks. Father Barry, on the scene, speaks to the men about the latest incident of the mob's "justice."

Monologue Two. Terry is served with a summons by the crime commission and is seen, on the street, talking casually with one of the commission investigators. Friendly tells Charley to bring his brother "back into line" or turn him over to the mob enforcers.

Charley picks Terry up in a cab and drives toward an address known to be mob territory. Realizing this, Terry starts out of the cab, but Charley pulls a gun. Terry gently guides the gun down, away from him. Charley is moved to recall that it must have been a former manager who brought Terry along too fast as a fighter, who ruined Terry's career. Charley says there must be a reason why Terry is acting this way—being disloyal to Friendly. Terry tells Charlie that isn't it.

Monologue One

FATHER BARRY

I came down here to keep a promise. I gave Kayo my word that if he stood up to the mob, I'd stand up with him—all the way. And now Kayo Dugan is dead. He was one of those fellows who had the gift for standing up. But this time they fixed him—oh—oh, they fixed him for good this time . . . unless it was an accident, like Big Mac says. Some people think the Crucifixion only took place on Calvary. They better wise up. Taking Joey Doyle's life to stop him from testifying is a crucifixion . . . and dropping a sling on Kayo Dugan because he was ready to spill his guts tomorrow—that's a crucifixion! And every time the mob puts the crusher on a good man—tries to stop him from doing his duty as a citizen—it's a crucifixion! And anybody who sits around and lets it happen—keeps silent about something he knows has happened—shares the guilt of it just as much as the Roman soldier who pierced the flesh of our Lord to see if he was dead!

[TRUCK

Go back to your church, Father!]

FATHER BARRY

Boys, this is my church! And if you don't think Christ is down here on the waterfront, you've got another guess coming! Every morning when the hiring boss blows his whistle, Jesus stands alongside you in the shape-up. He sees why some of you get picked and why some of you get passed over. He sees the family men worrying about getting their rent and getting food in the house for the wife and the kids. He sees you selling your soul to the mob for a day's pay! And what does Christ think of the easy-money boys who do none of the work and take all of the gravy? And how does he feel about the fellows who wear hundred-and-fifty-dollar suits and diamond rings on your union dues and your kickback money? And how does He, who spoke up without fear against every evil, feel about your silence? You want to know what's wrong with our waterfront? It's the love of a lousy buck. It's making love of a buck—the cushy job—more important than the love of man! It's forgetting that every fellow down here is your brother in Christ. But remember, Christ is always with you. Christ is in the shape-up—he's in the hatch—he's the union—he's kneeling right here beside Dugan—and he's staying with all of you. If you do it to the least of mine, you do it to me. And what they did to Joey and what they did to Dugan—they're doing to you—and you—you— All of you! And only you—only you with God's help have the power to knock them out for good! Okay, Kayo? Amen.

Monologue Two

TERRY

It wasn't him!
    (years of abuse crying out in him)
It was you, Charley. You and Johnny. Like the night the two of youse come in the dressing room and says, "Kid, this ain't your night—we're going for the price on Wilson." *It ain't my night.* I'd of taken Wilson apart that night! I was ready—remember the early rounds throwing them combinations. So what happens—this bum Wilson he gets the title shot—outdoors in the ball park!—and what do I get— a couple of bucks and a one-way ticket to Palookaville.
    (more and more aroused as he relives it)

It was you, Charley. You was my brother. You should of looked out for me. Instead of making me take them dives for the short-end money.

[CHARLEY
(defensively)
I always had a bet down for you. You saw some money.]

TERRY
(agonized)
See! You don't understand!

[CHARLEY
I tried to keep you in good with Johnny.]

TERRY
You don't understand! I could've been a contender. I could've had class and been somebody. Real class. Instead of a bum, let's face it, which is what I am. It was you, Charley.

La Strada

A Ponti/De Laurentiis Production, 1954
Screenplay by Federico Fellini, Ennio Flaiano,
and Tullio Pinelli
Directed by Federico Fellini

Time: An earlier time
Place: Italian countryside
This is Fellini's ardent, allegorical story of three wanderers on the back roads of the Italian countryside: an itinerant circus strongman, Zampano; a simpleminded, soulful girl, Gelsomina; and a creative, thoughtful clown, Il Matto.

Gelsomina, the young girl, is sold by her poor mother to Zampano, the traveling strongman, to be his cook (but she cannot cook) and assistant/clown in his "act." They try to make money by setting up their horse-drawn wagon and performing for the country folk. They fight. Zampano is gruff and insensitive, but they begin to need each other.

They join up, temporarily, with a small traveling circus, moving from village to village, and meet Il Matto, the circus's clever clown. Zampano and Il Matto eventually come to blows and are both thrown out of the circus for fighting.

At this point, after the fight, Il Matto and Gelsomina are talking. Gelsomina is confused about her feelings for Zampano, and speaks.

Gelsomina

I'll take matches . . . and I'll set fire to him . . . While he's driving, I set fire to the trailer, and all those dry clothes, the mattress, the blankets, and I'll burn up everything. I'll teach him! I never said, "No, I'm not going with that man." He gave ten thousand lire, I go to work. And him, he beats me! Is that the way to act?

(more emphatically)

He doesn't think. I tell him . . . and he . . . eh! Well, then, what's the use? But one of these days I'll poison his soup. "No," I said. I take matches and burn up everything. Or, I'll kill myself. To live this way! Why should you? We all get old, maybe we have to die, who knows how death is going to touch us, who knows about afterwards . . . If I go with them—

(nodding her head toward the circus wagons)

—it's the same thing. If I go back to Zampano, it's the same thing. So, I'm no good for anything. If I don't stay with him, who will?

The Night of the Hunter

United Artists (Produced by Paul Gregory), 1955
Screenplay by James Agee
Based on the novel by Davis Grubb
Directed by Charles Laughton

Time: 1930s, the Great Depression
Place: Ohio River country, U.S.A. A small village on the riverbank.
Times are hard along the Ohio River, in the small hamlets and towns hit by the Depression. A man, Ben Harper, driven by a need to feed his wife and family, steals $10,000, killing two men in the robbery. Pursued by the police, Harper hurriedly entrusts the money to his two young children, John and Pearl. He tells them to hide it and to promise *"never to tell"*—even their mother, Willa.

He's caught, imprisoned, and sentenced to hang. In jail he meets Preacher (Harry Powell) who is a self-proclaimed man of God, being held briefly for car theft. Preacher learns about the money before Ben is hanged.

In fact, Preacher is a con artist, thief, and murderer. As soon as he is released from prison Preacher, obsessed with finding the undiscovered money, heads for Harper's town. He plans to seduce Harper's widow to get the money.

The townspeople and the Harper family first meet Preacher at Spoon's Ice Cream Parlor. The adults accept and trust him, believing his masquerade. John, Harper's young son, is immediately suspicious, and he sees Preacher's tattooed hands. Preacher notices the fear and doubt in John's eyes and talks about the meaning of the markings on his hands.

PREACHER
Ah, little lad, you're staring at my fingers. Shall I tell you

the little story of Right-Hand-Left-Hand—the tale of Good and Evil? H-A-T-E!

(He thrusts up his left hand.)

It was with this left hand that old brother Cain struck the blow that laid his brother low! L-O-V-E!

(He thrusts up his right hand.)

See these here fingers, dear friends! These fingers has veins that lead straight to the soul of man! The right hand, friends! The hand of Love! Now watch and I'll show you the Story of Life. The fingers of these hands, dear hearts!—They're always a-tuggin' and a-warrin' one hand agin' t'other.

*(He locks his fingers and writhes them,
crackling the joints.)*

Look at 'em, dear hearts! Old Left Hand Hate's a-fightin' and it looks like Old Right Hand Love's a goner! But wait now! Hot dog! Love's a-winnin'! Yessirree! It's Love that won! Old Left Hand *Hate's* gone down for the count!

(He crashes both hands onto the table.)

The Goddess

Columbia Pictures (Produced by Milton Perlman), 1958
Screenplay by Paddy Chayefsky
Directed by John Cromwell

Time: Late 1940s
Place: Small Town, U.S.A.
Emily Ann Faulkner, a rural small-town girl in her teens, is the product of a lonely, unhappy childhood. She lives with her young, religious, widowed mother and dreams of escape and of being loved. She has fantasies of becoming a movie star, adored by everyone. When Emily acts in a

school play, she finally gets a response, something that feels like love, from her audience and her mother.

On a date with Lewis, a local boy, Emily Ann reveals her enthusiasm for the life of an actress in the following two monologues.

Monologue One

EMILY ANN

I sewed this I'm wearing myself, you know. Oh, I sew most of my clothes. I'm very good at that. I sewed the dress I wore in the show last month when the Dramatic Club, we did *Stage Door* by George Kaufman and Edna Ferber. Was you there? It was a triumph. Everybody said that was the best show the Dramatic Club has ever done. Everybody said it was just wonderful. Thelma Doris's mother said to me she never laughed so much in her life as the way I said my lines. It was a triumph!

(She is quite excited now, turned in her seat toward him, her eyes glowing.)

That was the most wonderful evening of my life. Was you there? Everybody just came over to me and was so nice. Miss Gillespie said I was the best girl she ever had in the Dramatic Club. Well, I was so scared. I was just saying words. I didn't know I was doing anything special. Everybody was so nice to me. I began to cry. Just all of a sudden I began to cry. Miss Gillespie, she said, "What are you crying about?" I said, "I don't know. Everybody's so nice to me." She said, "You should be happy. Tonight was a triumph for you." Well, I just couldn't stop bawling. My mother was there. She said, "What are you crying about?" I said, "I don't know." Well, I'm going to tell you, we went home, my mother and I—I just didn't want to go home at all that night. I was up in the clouds. But we finally went home, and my mother gave me a hug. And I began to cry all over again. My mother, you might know, is a Seventh-Day Adventist, and is very pious and severe, and she didn't even want me to be in the play. And we don't do much hugging in our house. I do believe that was the first hug she gave me in I don't remember—since I was an infant, I believe. She's a Seventh-Day Adventist, you know. She won't work on Saturday, not even in the defense plant down there where she's working now, in the Goodrich Rubber Company. All of a sudden in the last few years my mother has become very religious. She was a very pretty girl when she was young. My Uncle George says she was the belle of Clarksville, Tennessee. That's where I was born—that's near Fort Donelson, where Grant won the first Northern victory in the Civil War. Well, I couldn't stop crying all night long, and I woke up the next morning, I no sooner opened my eyes, and I began bawling again. I got tears in my eyes right now just talking about it. Isn't that the silliest thing you ever saw? That was the most wonderful night of my life.

Monologue Two

EMILY ANN
(bubbling with good humor)

Her real name isn't Ginger Rogers, you know. Her real name is Virginia McMath, and you know how she got started? She used to dance in Charleston contests, and somebody saw her, and that's how she became a star. I was thinking of taking dancing lessons, tap dancing and things like that, but they don't even have any place there in Hagerstown where they teach that. Do you know of any? Lana Turner was discovered in a drugstore, and there was one star—I think it was Priscilla Lane or Carole Landis—was just an old secretary, and she was riding up in the elevator, and this producer saw her and that's how she got her start. But I was talking about Ginger Rogers. I mean, she ain't like some of them stars. She don't go out to night clubs much, although there was one time there everybody thought she was going to marry Howard Hughes—it was in all the magazines. Anyway, she lives in a lovely home in Beverly Hills with her mother. She keeps her mother right there with her. I think that's nice. Ginger Rogers's dressing room has mirrors on the ceiling and the walls, and she has fruitwood furniture, and she loves classical music, you know? She's very close with Deems Taylor. He's a well-known classical musician. She has his picture on her wall, but there's no romance there in the wind, I don't think—just good friends.

(She has suddenly become aware that the boy
is turning the car into a side road.)

Where are we going, Lewis?

The Long, Hot Summer

Twentieth Century-Fox (Produced by Jerry Wald), 1958
Screenplay by Irving Ravetch and Harriet Frank, Jr.
Based on stories by William Faulkner
Directed by Martin Ritt

Time: 1958
Place: Frenchman's Bend, Mississippi
Ben Quick, a drifter in his early twenties, is followed by rumors that he is prone to arson. The rumors, however, have their roots in Ben's father, who was notorious for burning houses and barns in order to settle scores.

In a small town in rural Mississippi, Ben encounters Clara Varner, a teacher in her twenties who is considered to be fast closing in on spinsterhood. Clara's father,

Will (the richest and most important man in Frenchman's Bend), takes an immediate fatherly liking to Ben for two obvious reasons: He hopes that Ben will marry Clara, and he wants to incite the jealousy and ambition of his lazy son, Jody. Will even goes so far as to invite Ben to move into their house and work (as Jody's equal) in the Varner store.

Jody is overwhelmed by feelings of desperation at being passed over and ignored by his father, so he sets fire to a barn with Will trapped inside. He knows that Ben will, once again, become the automatic suspect. But he cannot let his father die, and rushes into the burning barn to rescue him.

As the fire rages, Clara suddenly, unexpectedly, helps Ben elude the townspeople who are pursuing him. Sitting in Clara's car, moments after evading the mob, Ben reveals his feelings about his past.

———————

BEN

I'm sick of that sight! I've seen fifty fires like that. Maybe a hundred. I've watched men with their shirts ablaze. I've seen horses cook. I grew up with the smell of gasoline around me, kerosene, coal oil, anything that would burn. My old man kept 'em in case he had a grudge he wanted to settle. My old man. My father.

(he pauses; then in a monotone)

The last time I saw him I was ten years old, lying in a ditch, crying my eyes out, praying that God would strike me dead. That was the night I'd run ahead to tell on him, to turn him in, to warn a farmer that he was coming with his torch. I remember choking on my own tears, and I remember a house burning, and I remember men on horseback and the sound of shots and my father running . . .

(sits beside her quietly a while)

Maybe those shots killed him. Maybe he died in one of the
fires he set. I don't know. I never saw him again.

[CLARA

How terrible for a boy of ten.]

BEN

The terrible part came later. Knocking around this whole
country, floating around from town to town, looking in
through other folks' kitchen windows from the outside . . .

(pause)

You see—that man left his mark on me. I've got his name.
And I can't run away from that.

Hiroshima Mon Amour

An Argos/Comei/Pathé/Daiei Production, 1959
Screenplay by Marguerite Duras
Directed by Alain Resnais

Time: August 1957
Place: Hiroshima, Japan
A French actress, about thirty years old, is in Hiroshima
to make a film. On her last day there she meets a Japanese
architectural engineer. Although each is married, with children, they fall in love.

Many years before, in the Nazi-occupied French village
of Nevers, her hometown, the actress had fallen in love
with a German soldier. He was shot during the Liberation,
and she was labeled a collaborator. As punishment by the
townspeople her head was shaved. She suffered a breakdown and could not control her screams, so her family put
her in their cellar to muffle her cries. When she emerged
from her cellar, apparently recovered, the first news she
heard was of the atomic explosion at Hiroshima.

Now, over ten ten years later, on the morning following their night of lovemaking, the actress and the Japanese engineer sit in a café. She tells her new lover of her experiences during the war.

SHE

We were supposed to meet at noon on the quays of the Loire. I was going to leave with him. When I arrived at noon on the quay of the Loire, he wasn't quite dead yet. Someone had fired on him from a garden.
(becoming delirious)
I stayed near his body all that day and then all the next night. The next morning they came to pick him up and they put him in a truck. It was that night Nevers was liberated. The bells of St. Etienne were ringing, ringing . . . Little by little he grew cold beneath me. Oh! how long it took him to die! When? I'm not quite sure. I was lying on top of him . . . yes . . . the moment of his death actually escaped me, because . . . because even at that very moment, and even afterward, yes, even afterward, I can say that I couldn't feel the slightest difference between this dead body and mine. All I could find between this body and mine were obvious similarities, do you understand?
(shouting)
He was my first love . . . And then one day . . . I had screamed again. So they put me back in the cellar.
(Her voice resumes its normal rhythm.)
It was warm . . .
(after a pause)
I think then is when I got over my hate.
(pause)
I don't scream anymore.
(pause)

I'm becoming reasonable. They say: "She's becoming reasonable."

(pause)

One night, a holiday, they let me go out. The banks of the
Loire. Dawn. People are crossing the bridge, sometimes
many, sometimes few, depending on the hour. From afar,
it's no one. Not long after that my mother tells me I have
to leave for Paris, by night. She gives me some money. I
leave for Paris, on a bicycle, at night. It's summer. The
nights are warm. When I reach Paris two days later the
name of Hiroshima is in all the newspapers. My hair is now
a decent length. I'm in the street with the people.

(as if she were waking up)

Fourteen years have passed. I don't even remember his
hands very well . . . The pain, I still remember the pain
a little.

The Apartment

United Artists/Mirisch (Produced by Billy Wilder), 1960
Screenplay by Billy Wilder and I. A. L. Diamond
Directed by Billy Wilder

Time: 1960
Place: Manhattan
This dark comedy is the story of C. C. (Bud) Baxter, an
employee at a large insurance firm, who is in his early
thirties, unmarried, and living alone in a small apartment
in Manhattan. He has little, if any, social life. Baxter has
been roped into letting his superiors—several married executives—use his apartment to carry on clandestine affairs
with various women. Because Baxter has "played ball" with
them, passing his apartment key from executive to exec-

utive, the executives "play ball" with Bud, recommending him to J. D. Sheldrake, the executive in charge of personnel, for an advance at the company.

Baxter moves to a junior executive position, complete with private office, but finds that Mr. Sheldrake, married for twelve years, is requesting the key to Bud's apartment. Sheldrake is having an affair with Fran Kubelik, who works as a white-gloved elevator operator in Baxter's office building. Fran is single, in her twenties, and lives with her sister and brother-in-law. Baxter is infatuated with Fran. They speak, make a date to meet one night at the theater, but Fran never shows up—she's with Sheldrake, at Baxter's apartment. Sweet-natured and vulnerable, Fran falls in love with Sheldrake and hopes he will divorce his wife. But at the office Christmas party someone tells Fran that she is only the latest in what has been a string of office affairs for Sheldrake.

At Bud's apartment on Christmas Eve, Sheldrake tells Fran that he cannot stay with her and must leave to be with his family. He hands her a hundred-dollar bill and tells her to get herself something nice for Christmas. Insulted, Fran takes the money and begins to undress—"as long as it's paid for"—but Sheldrake, in a hurry, rushes off, leaving Fran alone and despondent.

Fran attempts suicide in Bud's apartment. When Bud returns, he finds her there. He saves her life with the help of a neighbor who is a doctor. As she recovers, Fran and Bud exchange personal stories.

Monologue One

FRAN
(pensively)

I think I'm going to give it all up. Why do people have to love people, anyway? I don't want it. What do you call it when somebody keeps getting smashed up in automobile accidents? That's me with men. I've been jinxed from the word go—first time I was ever kissed was in a cemetery. I was fifteen—we used to go there to smoke. His name was George—he threw me over for a drum majorette. I just have this talent for falling in love with the wrong guy in the wrong place at the wrong time. The last one was manager of a finance company, back home in Pittsburgh— they found a little shortage in his accounts, but he asked me to wait for him—he'll be out in 1965. So I came to New York and moved in with my sister and her husband—he drives a cab. They sent me to secretarial school, and I applied for a job with Consolidated—but I flunked the typing test— Oh, I can type up a storm, but I can't spell. So they gave me a pair of white gloves and stuck me in an elevator—that's how I met Jeff— Oh, God, I'm so fouled up. What am I going to do now? Maybe he *does* love me— only he doesn't have the nerve to tell his wife.

Monologue Two

BUD

I know how you feel, Miss Kubelik. You think it's the end of the world—but it's not, really. I went through exactly the same thing myself. Well, maybe not *exactly*—I tried to do it with a gun. She was the wife of my best friend— and I was mad for her. But I knew it was hopeless—so I decided to end it all. I went to a pawnshop and bought a forty-five automatic and drove up to Eden Park—do you know Cincinnati? Anyway, I parked the car and loaded the gun—well, you read in the papers all the time that people shoot themselves, but believe me, it's not that easy—I mean, how do you do it?—here, or here, or here—
*(with cocked finger, he points to his temple,
mouth and chest)*

—you know where I finally shot myself?
            (*indicating knee*)
Here. While I was sitting there, trying to make my mind
up, a cop stuck his head in the car, because I was illegally
parked—so I started to hide the gun under the seat and it
went off—pow! Took me a year before I could bend my
knee—but I got over the girl in three weeks. She still lives
in Cincinnati, has four kids, gained twenty pounds—she
sends me a fruit cake every Christmas.
            (*shows it to her under Christmas tree*)
Here's the fruit cake. And you want to see my knee?

Elmer Gantry

United Artists (Produced by Bernard Smith), 1960
Screenplay by Richard Brooks
Based on the novel by Sinclair Lewis
Directed by Richard Brooks

Time: 1920s
Place: Midwest, U.S.A.
Elmer Gantry, in his thirties, is an articulate, smooth-talking
traveling salesman. Elmer likes his women and his liquor.
The film begins with Elmer in a bar during the Christmas
season, shooting the bull with some other salesmen. They
are approached by a woman begging money for an orphan-
age. Someone at the bar ridicules her request, pointing out
that religion "don't belong in a speakeasy."

Monologue One. Elmer is sympathetic to the woman
and seizes the opportunity to speak.

Not long after this, Elmer takes up with a traveling religious tabernacle led by Sister Sharon Falconer. Her evan-
gelical group moves from town to town, setting up their

tent and putting on a show calculated to save souls and raise money. Elmer's sales talents and charisma are well suited to this work.

In one town, however, a citizens' group protests the tabernacle's presence there. They are suspicious of corruption within the traveling evangelists' camp.

Elmer attempts to counteract these charges by mounting his own war on sin. He encourages the local police captain to raid a speakeasy. During the raid the police are about to arrest a number of prostitutes when Elmer spots an old girlfriend, Lulu Bains, among them. He tells the captain to run them out of town rather than put them in jail.

Monologue Two. Lulu had her first sexual experience with Elmer. Now in her thirties, she has encountered Elmer again. After he helps her avoid arrest Lulu calls Elmer to thank him and asks him up to her room.

Monologue One

GANTRY

Mac, wait a minute. Uhmmm-mmm. Excuse me sister, excuse me. Now don't tell me we're going to let these two little angels of mercy go away from here empty handed on Christmas eve? This joint is the home of fine bourbon and fast women . . . and we need plenty of religion to keep 'em both in line. So come on, folks, how about it? Get it up now, come on. Ah, come on, a little action here. A little— What's the matter? Ohhhh! Hey! Hey Lord! Can you hear me up there Jesus? You didn't think we'd forget your birthday, did you boy? There you are Jesus—and if I had any more you'd be welcome to it. Thank you brother. The Bible says never let your left hand know what your right hand is doing. Well, what's your beef, mister? You ashamed of being a Christian? Oh, I see. You think religion is for suckers and easy marks and mollycoddles, huh? You think Jesus

was some kind of sissy, eh? Well, let me tell you, Jesus
wouldn't be afraid to walk into this joint or any other speakeasy to preach the gospel. Jesus had guts! He wasn't afraid
of the whole Roman army. Think that quarterback's hot
stuff? Well, let me tell you . . . Jesus would have made
the best little all-American quarterback in the history of
football. Jesus was a real fighter. The best little scrapper
pound for pound you ever saw. And love, gentlemen? Love,
gentlemen. Jesus had love in both fists. And what is love?
Love is the mornin' and the evenin' star. It shines on the
cradle of the babe. Hey, ye sinners! Love is the inspiration
of poets and philosophers. Love is the voice of music. I'm
talking about divine love . . . not carnal love.

Monologue Two

LULU

Elmer, honey—baby—how could I put the squeeze on
you? Who's going to take the word of a five-buck hooker
against Elmer Gantry—I only wanted to see you for—well,
for— Gee, honey—look—look—I'm almost packed—the
cops gave me notice. I got a ticket on the midnight bus.
Ahh—I had no beef against you. I only wanted to see you
once more—kick around some old memories—maybe a
few laughs— Ah, who'm I kiddin'? When you first hit town
I figured you could go to hell anyway you wanted—without
my help. When you came bustin' in last night, like God
Almighty, wearing a tin star—I got mad, boilin' mad. All
I could think of was me—how you took me and ditched
me—that's all I could think of—me—little Miss Lulu, the
dumb pushover. When the cops said, "Get out of town in
twenty-four hours"—all I wanted to do is spit in your eye,
blackmail yuh, or shake yuh down, anything to hurt yuh.
But when you walked in just now—gee, honey—it was like

the first time between us, all over again—all goose pimples and— You'd better beat it.

(*sniffs*)

I'm—I'm sorry I phoned. I won't make any trouble— Not even if I could. Please go now. It's nobody's fault you ran out on me—except maybe my old man's. I heard from him last Christmas. The letter said:—"Daughter, read First Kings, Chapter Twenty-one, Verse Twenty-three." I looked it up. It said—"And the dogs in the street shall eat Jezebel—" Hmmm. My old man and his Bible. Tell me—how is it some people can only find hate in the Bible . . . ?

Breakfast at Tiffany's

Paramount Pictures (Produced by Martin Jurow
and Richard Shepherd), 1961
Screenplay by George Axelrod
Based on the novel by Truman Capote
Directed by Blake Edwards

Time: 1961
Place: Manhattan
Holly Golightly is a self-created party girl, a strange combination of sophisticated style and eccentric, often childlike tastes. She likes to give the impression that she's seen and done it all, but when the truth is told, Holly is revealed to be Lulamae Barnes, a poor, uneducated country girl from Tulip, Texas. A child bride, Holly ran away from her older husband, Doc, and his children.

Now in New York, Holly stays up all night and hits the frenetic hot spots that make up the social scene in the city. She strikes up a relationship with Paul Varjak, a promising

writer in his twenties who is Holly's upstairs neighbor in
their Upper East Side brownstone.

Monologue Two. Holly has met Jose, a fabulously wealthy
landowner from Brazil, who proposes marriage. She talks
to Paul about Jose.

Monologue One. Paul has been invited to his first big
party at Holly's apartment. There he meets O. J. Berman,
Holly's agent and bemused protector. Paul asks O. J. if he's
known Holly long.

Monologue One

O. J.

Known her long? Me . . . O. J. Berman . . . I'm the one
discovered her! On the coast, a couple of years ago, out at
Santa Anita. She's hanging around the track. The kid's just
fifteen. But stylish. Even though when she opens her mouth,
you don't know if she's a hill-billy or an okie or what. One
year it took to smooth out that accent. How we finally did
it, we give her French lessons. After that she gradually
learns to imitate English. Finally, when I think she's ready—
I set her up with a screen test . . . I could kill myself . . . the night before . . . wham! The phone rings! She
says: This is Holly. I say: Baby, you sound far away. She
says: I'm in New York. I say: What kind of New York? You
got a screen test here tomorrow. She says: I'm in New York
because I've never been to New York. I say: Get your butt
on a plane and get back here. She says: I don't want it. I
say: You don't want it? She says: I don't want it. I say: What
do you want? She says: When I find out, you'll be the first
one to now. So, listen, Fred-baby . . .

[PAUL

Paul-baby . . .]

O. J.

Don't stand there and try to tell me she ain't a phony.

Monologue Two

HOLLY

Look, I know what you think. And I don't blame you, I've always thrown out such a jazzy line. But really . . . except for Doc . . . and you . . . Jose is my first non-rat romance. Oh, not that he's my ideal of the absolute finito. He tells little lies and worries about what people think and he wants to be the President of Brazil . . . I mean it's such a *useless* thing for a grown man to want to be . . . and he takes about fifty baths a day . . . I think a man should smell . . . at least a *little bit.* No, he's too prim and cautious to be my absolute ideal. If I were free to choose from anybody alive . . . just snap my fingers and say "Come here, you!" . . . I wouldn't pick Jose. Nehru maybe . . . or Adlai Stevenson or Sidney Poitier or Leonard Bernstein . . . but I *do* love Jose. I honestly think I'd give up *smoking* if he asked me to!

Jules and Jim

Films du Carrose/SEDIF (Produced by Marcel Berbert), 1961
Screenplay by Francois Truffaut and Jean Gruault
Based on the novel by Henri-Pierre Roche
Directed by François Truffaut

Time: 1912–1920s
Place: Paris and environs and the southern French countryside
In pre–World War I, bohemian Paris, Jules, an Austrian, and Jim, a Frenchman, both in their twenties, meet and become friends. Racing from café to bistro, they are in search of beauty, danger, and fantasy. They meet Catherine. She is what they're both looking for. She's impulsive, mysterious, and beautiful. Catherine, a Frenchwoman, teaches Shakespeare. Her mother was a lower-class Eng-

lishwoman, her father a French aristocrat.

Catherine marries Jules. World War I separates the men, but after the war they renew and maintain their friendship. Catherine has had Jules's child, Sabine, but takes other lovers, as she always has. Jules, sensing that he does not totally satisfy all of Catherine's needs, invites Jim to visit them. He hopes that by bringing Jim back into their lives, Catherine will be happier. Jim is having a quiet ongoing love affair with a woman, Gilberte, but still finds himself attracted to Catherine. He senses all is not well between Catherine and Jules.

Monologue One. In a conversation during this visit Catherine tells Jim about her love life, past and current.

Monologue Two. Later, during an outing in the country, Jim, Jules, and Albert, Catherine's current lover, are sitting under trees talking. Jules mentions that Albert had been wounded in the war. Jim recalls a story told to him during the war.

Monologue One

CATHERINE

I will start the story again from the beginning, as I have lived it myself. It was Jules's generosity, his innocence, his vulnerability which dazzled me, conquered me. He was so different from other men. By giving him happiness, I hoped to cure him of these crises where he felt lost and out of his depth. But I realised that these crises are an inseparable part of him. Our happiness, for we were happy, did not last, and there we were, face to face, linked together. His family was sheer purgatory for me. On the eve of our wedding, during a reception, Jules's mother wounded me deeply by her clumsy behaviour. Jules remained passive—which was tantamount to condoning it. I punished him immediately by taking up with an old lover, Harold . . . *Yes, lover.*

That way I would be quits with Jules, when we were married; we could start again from scratch. Fortunately, the family has gone to live in the north, I don't know where. War broke out; Jules went off east. He wrote me marvelous, passionate love-letters. I loved him more at a distance. Once again, I saw him with a halo. Our final misunderstanding, the real rupture, came on his first leave. I felt I was in the arms of a stranger. He went off again. Sabine was born nine months later. You can think what you like . . . she is his. But I said to him: "I have given you a daughter; that is enough for me. This chapter is closed. Let's sleep in separate rooms . . . I am taking back my liberty."

(a pause)

Do you remember our young friend, Fortunio? He was there, as free as air . . . and so was I. He was kind, he made a good partner. What a holiday we had! But he was too young; it wasn't a serious affair. And one fine day, to my surprise . . . I found I missed Jules's indulgent and leisurely ways. I felt drawn back to my daughter like a magnet. I was on the wrong track. So I left. I have only been back here three months. Jules is finished for me as a husband. Don't be sorry for him. I still allow him the distractions he needs . . . Then there is Albert. He has told me about the statue which the three of you fell in love with, and which I apparently look like. I've flirted with him. There are some bizarre sides to his character, but he has the natural authority which Jules lacks. He wants me to leave everything, to marry him. He would take the mother and daughter together. I like him a lot, but nothing more—so far. Anyway, he is coming to lunch tomorrow. I shall see. You've been a good listener, I have talked more than you. I don't claim to have said everything, no more than you just now. Perhaps I have had other lovers; that's my affair. I have only talked about things which you mentioned yourself . . . It's almost dawn now.

Monologue Two

JIM

I am thinking of a gunner I knew at the hospital. He was
coming back from leave when he met a young girl on the
train. They talked to each other all the way from Nice to
Marseilles. As she stepped out onto the platform, she gave
him her address. Then, for two years he wrote to her fre-
netically every day from the trenches, on bits of wrapping
paper, by candle-light. He kept on writing even when the
mortar bombs were raining down around him, and his letters became more and more intimate in tone. At first he
began "Dear Mademoiselle," and ended "With all good
wishes." In the third letter, he called her "My little sylph,"
and asked her for a photograph . . . Then it was "My adorable sylph," then "I kiss your hands," then "I kiss your
forehead." Later on, he described the photograph she had
sent him and talked about her bosom, which he thought
he could see under her *peignoir,* and soon he dropped the
formal mode of address and started to call her "tu": "Je
t'aime terriblement." One day, he wrote to the girl's mother
asking for her hand and became officially engaged to her,
although he hardly knew her. The war went on and the
letters became more and more intimate. "I take hold of
you, my love, I take your adorable breasts . . . I press you
against me quite naked . . ." When she replied rather coldly
to one of his letters, he flew into a passion and begged
her . . . not to flirt with him because he might die from
one day to the next. And he was right.

(a pause)

You see, Jules, to understand this extraordinary deflow-
ering by correspondence, one must have experienced all
the violence of the war in the trenches, its particular kind
of collective madness, with death constantly present. So
there was a man who, at the same time as taking part in

the Great War, managed to conduct his own little parallel war, his individual struggle, and completely conquer the heart of a woman from a distance. When he arrived at the hospital, he was wounded in the head like you, but he wasn't as lucky as you. He died after being trepanned, just the day before the armistice. In his last letter to the fiancée he hardly knew, he wrote: "Your breasts are the only bombs I love." I'll show you a series of photographs I have of him . . . If one looks at them quickly, one has the illusion that he is moving.

The Hustler

Twentieth Century-Fox (Produced by Robert Rossen), 1961
Screenplay by Robert Rossen and Sidney Carroll
Based on the novel by Walter Tevis
Directed by Robert Rossen

Time: 1961
Place: Small Town, U.S.A., and City, U.S.A.
Eddie Felson is a pool shark. He makes his living by beating unsuspecting players around back-room pool tables in small towns and cities.

Eddie meets his match, however, in a game against the legendary master, Minnesota Fats. Overconfident and dizzy with his prowess, Eddie tires, gets sloppy, and loses the all-night marathon game.

He catches the eye, though, of a big time gambler/manager, Bert Gordon. Gordon tells Eddie that while he's a good player, he's a loser because he hasn't got enough character to win over Fats. Eddie drops his old manager and takes up with Gordon, who's got connections at big-time games.

Eddie has recently met and moved in with Sarah Packard, an ex-actress and part-time college student. She has a slight limp and a serious drinking problem. She and Eddie develop a stormy, passionate and, at times, caring relationship.

Monologue One. Eddie has had his thumbs broken by some sore losers. Sarah sobers up to take care of him as his hands heal. They go to a park by the river near Sarah's city apartment to have a picnic. Sarah asks Eddie if losing bothers him.

Monologue Two. Eddie becomes torn between life with Sarah and the life of a pool shark with Gordon. Gordon takes Eddie to Louisville to play against a rich gambling man, and Sarah goes along, disapproving. In his hotel room in Louisville, Gordon tells Sarah that Eddie wants her to go, and then Gordon tries to seduce her. At first she rejects his advances but then, on a blind, self-destructive impulse, she returns to Gordon's room and sleeps with him. Afterward Sarah goes into his bathroom, scrawls "perverted, twisted, crippled" on the mirror and kills herself. When Eddie discovers her body, he attacks Gordon.

Finally Eddie goes back to play Minnesota Fats and this time wins. After the match he encounters Gordon, who tries to explain that Sarah would have killed herself sooner or later—she was that kind of woman. Eddie responds.

Monologue One

EDDIE
(after a pause)

Yeah. It bothers me a lot. 'Cause you see, twice, Sarah—once at Ames with Minnesota Fats and then again at Arthur's—in that cheap, crummy poolroom . . . Now, why did I do it, Sarah? Why did I do it? I coulda beat that guy, I coulda beat him cold. He never woulda known. But I just had to show 'em, I just had to show those creeps and those punks what the game is like when it's great, when it's really great. You know, like anything can be great. Anything can be great . . . I don't care . . . Bricklaying can be great. If a guy knows. If he knows what he's doing and why, and if he can make it come off. I mean, when I'm goin'—I mean when I'm really goin'—I feel like, like what a jockey must feel. He's sittin' on his horse, he's got all that speed and that power underneath him, he's comin' into the stretch and the pressure's on him—and he knows. Just feels, when to let go, and how much. So he's got everything working for him—timing, touch. It's a great feeling, boy, it's a really great feeling when you're right, and you know you're right. Like all of sudden I got oil in my arm. Pool cue is a part of me. You know, pool cue has got nerves in it. It's a piece of wood but it's got nerves in it. You can feel the roll of those balls. You don't have to look. You just know. You make shots that nobody's ever made before. And you play that game the way nobody ever played it before. You know, someday, Sarah, you're gonna settle down. You're gonna marry a college professor and you're gonna write a great book. Maybe about me, huh? Fast Eddie Felson, hustler.

Monologue Two

EDDIE

We really stuck the knife into her didn't we, Bert?

[BERT

(disgustedly)

Aaaahhhh!]

EDDIE

Boy, we really gave it to her good.

[BERT

If it didn't happen in Louisville, it'd happen someplace else. If it didn't happen now, it'd happen six months from now. That's the kinda dame she was.]

EDDIE

And we twisted it, didn't we, Bert? But maybe that doesn't stick in your throat 'cause you spit it out just like you spit out everything else. But it sticks in mine. I loved her, Bert. I traded her in on a pool game. But that wouldn't mean anything to you. Because who did you ever care about? Just win, win, you said, win . . . that's the important thing. You don't know what winnin' is, Bert. You're a loser. 'Cause you're dead inside, and you can't live unless you make everything else dead around you.

(FATS listens, his head bowed.)

Too high, Bert. The price is too high. Because if I take it, she never lived, she never died. And we both know that's not true, don't we, Bert? She lived, she died. Boy, you better . . . You tell your boys they better kill me, Bert. They better go all the way with me. Because if they just bust me up, I'll put all those pieces back together, and so help me, so help me God, Bert . . . I'm gonna come back here and I'm gonna kill you.

To Kill a Mockingbird

Universal-International (Produced by Alan Pakula), 1962
Screenplay by Horton Foote
Based on the novel by Harper Lee
Directed by Robert Mulligan

Time: 1962
Place, Macomb, Alabama
To Kill a Mockingbird is the story of Atticus Finch, a widower in his forties, and his two children: son Jem, thirteen; and daughter Scout, six. Atticus is a lawyer who has chosen to defend a black man, Tom Robinson, on trial for allegedly

raping a white girl. The girl, Mayella Ewell, is in her early twenties and is described by the screenwriter as a "thick-bodied white girl, accustomed to strenuous labor."

Monologue One. Mayella Ewell takes the stand to testify against Tom Robinson. It has been made clear to her by her bullying father that if she doesn't accuse Tom of raping her, he will beat her.

Monologue Two. Atticus gives his summation to the jury.

Monologue One

MAYELLA

Well, sir, I was on the porch and . . . and he came along and, you see, there was this old chiffarobe in the yard, Papa'd brought in to chop up for kindlin'. Papa told me to do it while he was off in the woods, but I wasn't feelin' strong enough then, so he came by and I said, "Come here, nigger, and bust up this chiffarobe and I'll give you a nickel," and I turn around and 'fore I know it, he was on me. I fought'n hollered but he had me around the neck. He hit me again and again. Next thing I knew, Papa was in the room a-standin' over me hollerin', "Who done it, who done it?" . . . That nigger yonder took advantage of me, an' if you fine, fancy gentlemen don't wanna do nothin' about it, then you're all yellow, stinkin' cowards, the lot of you. Your fancy airs don't come to nothin'. Your Ma'am-in' and Miss Mayellerin' don't come to nothin', Mr. Finch.

Monologue Two

ATTICUS

Gentlemen, I shall be brief, but I would like to use my remaining time with you to remind you that this case is not a difficult one, it requires no minute sifting of complicated facts, but it does require you to be sure beyond all reasonable doubt as to the guilt of the defendant. To begin with, this case should never have come to trial. The state has not produced one iota of medical evidence to the effect that the crime Tom Robinson is charged with ever took place. It has relied instead upon the testimony of two witnesses whose evidence has not only been called into serious question on cross examination, but has been flatly contradicted by the defendant. The defendant is not guilty but somebody in this courtroom is. There is circumstantial evidence to indicate that Mayella Ewell was beaten savagely by someone who led almost exclusively with his left . . . and Tom Robinson now sits before you, having taken the oath with the only good hand he possesses—his right hand. In this country our courts are the great levelers, and in our courts all men are created equal. I'm no idealist to believe firmly in the integrity of our courts and in the jury system. That is no ideal to me . . . it is a living, working reality. Gentlemen, a court is no better than each man of you sitting before me on this jury. A court is only as sound as its jury, and a jury is only as sound as the men who make it up. I am confident that you gentlemen will review without passion the evidence you have heard, come to a decision and restore this defendant to his family. In the name of God, do your duty. In the name of God, believe Tom Robinson.

Freud

Universal-International (Produced by
Wolfgang Rheinhardt), 1963
Screenplay by Charles Kaufman and Wolfgang Rheinhardt
Directed by John Huston

Time: 1890s

Place: Vienna

Sigmund Freud is a young doctor in his thirties. He journeys to Paris to study the uses of hypnosis to cure hysteria and various nervous disorders.

Freud returns to Vienna and begins working with Dr. Breuer, who has been treating a young woman named Cecily. Cecily had a complete nervous breakdown about a year ago following the death of her father. She now suffers from insomnia, paralysis, and, at times, hysterical blindness.

Cecily's father died in the arms of a prostitute. Cecily identified her father at the site of his death. When Dr. Breuer is forced to stop treating Cecily, Freud takes over the case.

Monologue One. Under Freud's care, Cecily relates a dream she had.

Monologue Two. Mrs. Koertner, Cecily's mother, now in her forties, a cabaret dancer before her marriage, confides in Dr. Freud.

Monologue One

CECILY

I was walking along by the seashore and suddenly I saw a tall, round, red tower. There was an inscription above the entrance and a coat of arms. A funny one. A staff with a snake wound around it. There was a woman, her body was

painted with marvelous images. She could have been an
Egyptian. A tall, handsome man came up to her in full
evening dress. The woman said, "I'm Frau Putipar." She
tried to fit on the man's finger a wedding band of the thin-
nest metal, but his own gold ring prevented it. Hers rolled
off and slipped away. At that the man turned and ran. He
stumbled and fell to the ground as if dead. I ran to help
him, but when I got there I found only a heap of clothes.
A window in the tower opened and a woman looked out.
It was my mother. She pointed threateningly to the painted
girl and said, "Blood will tell, my girl. It can't be washed
out, no matter what you do."

Monologue Two

FRAU KOERTNER

Cecily's asleep. I would like to talk to you. Forgive me. I
haven't cried for a long time. She talked in her sleep last
night as she used to when she was little. She used to wake
up screaming and say that she had dreamed that I was dead.
There was a time when I wished she was dead. When I
carried her in my womb I did. Before I was married I was
a dancer in a cheap cabaret. You know the legend—Leda
and the Swan? That is what I danced. I wore one long white
glove that looked like the head and neck of a swan and very
little else. One night, after doing my turn, I came back to
my dressing room and found a man sitting there. A handsome swell, with a flower in his buttonhole. Six weeks later
we were married. We creatures, as everyone knows, long
for respectability. I only wanted to forget the past. Be a
good wife and mother. I was pregnant before the honey-
moon was over but I waited to tell Joseph until our first
night home. We dined alone and I chose a simple dress for
the occasion and wore no jewelry except a wedding ring.

But everything went wrong. He drank too much . . . He didn't like my dress. He said, "Take off that drab thing, Leda, and dance for me the way you used to." Finally I blurted out my news. I'll never forget the look on his face. Without a word he rose and left the house to go and look for another Leda, and another and another. He never touched me again. He had married me only to have a harlot in the house. From that time on I was alone. His friends never called when I was alone, nor did they receive me. He visited them alone and later with Cecily. There was a time when I was away for several weeks that the two of them entertained half of Vienna.

Dr. Strangelove

Columbia Pictures (Produced by Stanley Kubrick), 1963
Screenplay by Stanley Kubrick, Terry Southern,
and Peter George
Based on the novel *Red Alert,* by Peter George
Directed by Stanley Kubrick

Time: 1964
Place: Washington, D.C.
In this satiric comedy about a nuclear showdown, the commander of Burpleson Air Force Base, General Jack Ripper, has issued orders to thirty-four B-52 fighter jets (the 843rd Bomb Wing) to attack their targets inside Russia. Each B-52 can deliver a bomb load of fifty megatons, sixteen times the explosive force of all the bombs and shells used by all the armies in World War II.

Wing Attack Plan R is under way. Plan R is an emergency war plan in which a lower echelon officer (like General

Ripper) can order nuclear retaliation after a sneak attack has occurred on Washington and the normal chain of command is disrupted.

The Russians have not attacked Washington or any other city. Ripper just *thinks* they will. He's decided that war should not be left up to the politicians but to men like him. Jack Ripper is crazy. He's sealed the base from all communications and will shoot to kill any forces, American or otherwise, that try to break into the base and cancel the attack. The pilots think that Washington has been leveled and have switched their radios to a special frequency that can only receive messages preceded by a particular three-letter code, effectively shutting off all communication with the outside world.

There's only one man in the world who knows the code— Ripper—and he's locked in his base, babbling. There are seventeen thousand permutations for the three-letter code. It would take two days for someone to figure it out, and the planes are less than two hours from their targets in Russia.

The President of the United States meets with his Joint Chiefs of Staff in the war room to discuss the crisis. He orders his staff to get the Premier of Russia, Premier Kisoff, on the hot line. The President talks to the Premier.

PRESIDENT

Hello . . . Eh, hello, Di— Hello, Dimitri. Listen, I—I can't hear too well, do you suppose you could turn the music down just a little. Ah, ah, that's much better. Yes, huh, yes. Fine, I can hear you now, Dimitri, clear and plain and coming through fine. I'm coming through fine too, eh? Good, then, well, then as you say, we're both coming through fine. Good. Well, it's good that you're fine then, and I'm fine. I agree with you, it's great to be fine.

(laughs)

Now then, Dimitri, you know how we've always talked about the possibility of something going wrong with the bomb. The bomb, Dimitri, the hydrogen bomb. Well now, what happened is, uh, one of our base commanders, he had a sort of, well, he went a little funny in the head. You know, just a little funny. And—uh—he went and did a silly thing. Well, I'll tell you what he did. He ordered his planes to attack your country. Uh—Well, let me finish, Dimitri . . . Let me finish, Dimitri. Well, listen, how do you think I feel about it? Can you imagine how I feel about it, Dimitri? Why do you think I'm calling you? Just to say hello? Of course I like to speak to you. Of course I like to say hello. Not now, but any time, Dimitri. I'm just calling up to tell you something terrible has happened. It's a friendly call, of course it's a friendly call. Listen, if it wasn't friendly you probably wouldn't have even got it. They will not reach their targets for at least another hour. I am, I am positive, Dimitri. Listen, I've been all over this with your Ambassador, it is not a trick. Well, I'll tell you. We'd like to give your Air Staff a complete rundown on the targets, the flight plans and the defensive systems of the planes. Yes, I mean, if—if—if we're unable to recall the planes then I'd say that—uh—well, we're just going to—uh—have to help you destroy them, Dimitri. I know they're our boys. All right. Well, listen, now who should we call? Who should we call, Dimitri, the—what was—the people—sorry, you faded away there. The People's Central Air Defense Headquarters. Where is that, Dimitri? In Omsk. Right. Yes . . . Oh, you'll call them first, will you? Uh-huh. Listen, do you happen to have the phone number on you, Dimitri? Well . . . what? I see, just ask for Omsk Information. Uh-uh-hmm. I'm sorry too, Dimitri. I'm very sorry. All right, you're sorrier than I am, but I am sorry as well. I am as sorry as you are, Dimitri, don't say that you're more sorry than I am because

I'm capable of being just as sorry as you are. So we're both sorry, all right? All right. Yes, he's right here. Yes, he wants to talk to you, just a second.

Inside Daisy Clover

Warner Brothers and Pakula-Mulligan Productions, 1965
Screenplay by Gavin Lambert, from his novel
Directed by Robert Mulligan

Time: 1930s
Place: Hollywood and environs
A young girl named Daisy Clover has sent her do-it-yourself record to be evaluated by pros in Hollywood. Raymond Swan and his wife, Melora, star-makers at a major film studio, discover the record and decide to turn Daisy into a star. Daisy's career takes off, and she meets and marries Wade Lewis, Hollywood's biggest heartthrob. Wade, however, is homosexual, and their strained marriage, combined with the pressures of life in Hollywood, cause Daisy to suffer a nervous breakdown. Swan talks with her as she recovers.

SWAN
You may as well know the rest.
(almost to himself)
Two people can sleep around but stay together. We all like a change. That's what vacations are for.
(directly to DAISY)
But when one of them gets romantic about it—carries on about true love and deep understanding, a wonderful new person opening doors for her . . .

(breaks off impatiently)

All the good women and all the good men who try to put Wade back together again . . . Like most causes, nobody wants to give him up. Age and sex don't matter—take him to heart and he'll take you to bed. He really had fun with you . . . But then, like the others, you needed him—and you woke up alone.

(pause)

I told Melora she didn't stand a chance. I told her what would happen. It happened. She cut her wrists and blamed *me*.

(SWAN looks back at DAISY. She hasn't moved, hasn't visibly reacted.)

It appears I lack the finer points—but Wade's got them all. Thousands of girls sit watching him in dark movie theatres, go home and dream about him in dark little bedrooms. Thousands of wives wish their husbands were exactly like him . . .

(chuckles)

Isn't that something? You can't help admiring the man.

(pause)

I just signed him for three more pictures.

(DAISY reacts.)

He's in New York on vacation. Be back in two weeks.

(stands close over her)

I'll see you don't run into each other. No more problems. You've got the best divorce lawyer in town.

(DAISY looks away from SWAN, stares at the pool again.)

Are *you* blaming me, too?

(no answer)

If I'd warned you about Wade, you'd have called it a wicked lie. And Wade would have said, "The Prince of Darkness stops at nothing, dear heart."

(looks wry for a moment)

You'd have eloped immediately.
> (*DAISY looks at him for a moment, looks away
> again.*)

The worst is over. Sleep it off, Daisy. Take a long deep
sleep.
> (*no reaction*)

Sandman's orders.
> (*DAISY still doesn't react. SWAN picks her up,
> like a father carrying a child.*)

The Pawnbroker

Landau-Unger (Produced by Worthington Minse), 1965
Screenplay by David Friedkin and Morton Fine
Based on the novel by Edward Lewis Wallant
Directed by Sidney Lumet

Time: August 1, 1963
Place: Spanish Harlem, New York City
Sol Nazerman, forty-five years old, is a survivor of Auschwitz. Twenty years ago Sol's wife, Ruth, and their children,
Naomi and David, died at Auschwitz. Before the war, Sol
was a professor at the University of Cracow, but now he
runs a pawnship in Spanish Harlem. He has an apprentice,
Jesus Ortiz, a Puerto Rican kid of about twenty who helps
Sol take care of the store and runs errands for him.

One evening Jesus asks Sol, "How come you people come
to business so naturally?" Sol, usually a private man of few
words, responds.

SOL

You begin . . . you begin with several thousand years dur-

ing which you have nothing except a great bearded legend.
Nothing else. You have no land to grow food on. No land
on which to hunt. Not enough time in one place to have a
geography, or an army, or a land-myth. You have only a
little brain in your head and this bearded legend to sustain
you . . . convince you there is something special about you,
even in your poverty. But this little brain . . . that is the
real key. With it you obtain a small piece of cloth, wool,
silk, cotton—it doesn't matter. You take this cloth and you
cut it in two and sell the two pieces for a penny or two
more than you paid for the one. With this money, then,
you buy a slightly larger piece of cloth. Which perhaps may
be cut into three pieces. And sold for three pennies profit.
You must never succumb to buying an extra piece of bread
at this point. Or a toy for your child. Immediately you must
go out and buy a still larger cloth, or two large cloths. And
repeat the process. And so you continue until there is no
longer any temptation to dig in the earth and grow food.
No longer any desire to gaze at limitless land which is in
your name. You repeat this process over and over for centuries and centuries. And then, all of a sudden, you discover
you have a mercantile heritage. You are known as a mer-
chant. You're also known as a man with secret resources,
usurer, pawnbroker, a witch, or what have you.

(pause)

But by then it is instinct. Do you understand?

Persona

Svensk Filmindustri (Produced by Lars-Owe Carlberg), 1966
Screenplay by Ingmar Bergman
Directed by Ingmar Bergman

Time: 1966

Place: Well-appointed beach house on the Swedish seacoast

Elisabeth Vogler, an accomplished and acclaimed actress in her thirties, while performing on stage as Electra, is suddenly struck mute. While there is nothing wrong with her physically, she will not utter a single word. She is treated by a psychiatrist, a woman. Because Elisabeth's silence persists, the doctor eventually sends her to the doctor's seaside summer house to rest and recuperate.

Elisabeth seems to be overwhelmed by the death, evil, and injustice in the world, the superficiality of everyday life and her own profession. There is nothing for her to say in the face of this reality. She even tears apart a photograph of her young child sent to her by her husband.

The doctor entrusts Elisabeth's care to a young, pretty nurse, Alma, who is there at the beach house to be a friendly, supportive companion during the healing process. In Elisabeth's silence Alma begins to speak, naturally at first, about herself, to gain Elisabeth's interest and trust. Soon Alma begins to reveal more and more intimate details and secrets of her life—her relationship with her fiancé, Karl Henrik, her teenage sexual experiences, her abortion. Elisabeth draws Alma out with her silence. Alma is twenty-five years old. Her parents have a farm, and her mother was a nurse before she was married.

Alma, in ever frustrated curiosity about what Elisabeth is thinking, opens a letter from Elisabeth to her doctor and feels betrayed and hurt as she reads Elisabeth's comments. Elisabeth has written to her doctor about details of Alma's confessional conversations. Alma had actually begun to become quite attached to Elisabeth.

In this monologue Alma confronts Elisabeth with this discovery and her pent-up frustrations at Elisabeth's behavior.

ALMA

Would you do something for me? I know it's asking a lot, but I could do with your help.

(ELISABETH looks up from her book. She has been listening to ALMA's tone of voice and, for a moment, there is a trace of fear in her eyes.)

It's nothing dangerous. But I do wish you could *talk to me.* I don't mean anything special. We could talk about the weather, for instance. Or what we're going to have for dinner, or whether the water's going to be cold after the storm. Cold enough to stop us going in. Can't we talk for a few minutes? Or just for a minute? Or you read me something from your book. Just say a couple of words.

(ALMA is still standing with her back to the wall, her head leaned forward, the black sunglasses on her nose.)

It's not easy to live with someone who doesn't say anything, I promise you. It spoils everything. I can't bear to hear Karl-Henrik's voice on the telephone. He sounds so artificial. I can't talk to him any more, it's so unnatural. You hear your own voice too and *no one else!* And you think, "Don't I sound false." All these words I'm using. Look, now I'm talking to you, I can't stop, but I hate talking because I still can't say what I want. But you've made things simple for yourself, you just shut up. No, I must try not to get angry. You don't say anything, that's your business, I know. But just now *I need* you to talk to me. Please, please, can't you talk to me, just a bit! It's almost unbearable.

(A long pause. ELISABETH shakes her head.
ALMA smiles, as if she were trying not to cry.)
I knew you'd say no. Because you can't know how I feel.
I always thought that great artists had this tremendous
feeling of sympathy for other people. That . . . they created
out of sympathy with people, from a need to help them.
Silly of me.
(She takes off her glasses and puts them in her
pocket. ELISABETH sits there, anxious and
immobile.)
Use it and throw it away. You've used me—I don't know
what for—and now you don't need me anymore you're
throwing me away.
(ALMA is about to go into the house, but stops
on the threshold, and gives a subdued howl of
desperation.)
Yes, I know, I can hear perfectly well how artificial it sounds.
"You don't need me any more and you're throwing me
away." That's what's happened to me. Every word. And
these glasses!
(She takes her glasses from her pocket and
throws them down on the terrace. Then she
sinks down onto the steps.)
No, I'm just hurt, that's all. I'm out of my mind with misery
and disappointment. You've done me such harm. You laughed
at me behind my back. You're a devil, an absolute devil.
People like you ought to be shot. You're mad. Just think,
I read that letter of yours to the doctor, where you laugh
at me. Just imagine, I did that, it was still open and I've
got it here, I never sent it and I promise you I've really
read it. And you got me to talk. You got me to tell you
things that I've never said to anyone. And you just pass it
on. What a case history for you. Isn't it? You can't do it—
you can't!

*(She suddenly comes up, grabs ELISABETH's
arms and starts shaking her.)*

Now you're going to talk. Have you anything—now, my
God, I'm going to make you talk to me!

In the Heat of the Night

United Artists/Mirisch (Produced by Walter Mirisch), 1967
Screenplay by Stirling Silliphant
Directed by Norman Jewison

Time: 1967, summer afternoon
Place: Sparta, Mississippi
Delores Purdy is a pregnant sixteen-year-old who accuses
Sam Ward, a police deputy, of being the father of her child.
Sam is also a suspect in a local murder case. The murder
investigation is being headed by Sparta's police chief, Gil-
lespie, and Virgil Tibbs, a black homicide expert from Phil-
adelphia.

Delores's brother has dragged Delores into the police
station to tell her story to Chief Gillespie.

Virgil remains in the room, despite Purdy's protests.
Delores tells her story to the three men.

DELORES

You know how hot it's been? Nights . . . they're no better.
My brother works nights. Leaves me all alone. This particular night I go out on the porch . . . thinking how nice
it'd be to have a fountain drink. Sam comes down the
road . . . like he does every night . . . passing like a lord
in his fine, big shiny car! But this time he stops. He's got

a nice face, don't you think, Chief. He says . . . "Hey, little girl . . . you know what's the coolest spot in town?" "No Sam," I said. "I guess I don't." And he said—"The cemetery, that's where. Know why? Because they got all them big cool tombstones. You ever stretch out on a tombstone, Delores? Feel all that nice cool marble along your body?" So . . . I went for a ride with him . . . to the cemetery.

Easy Rider

Columbia/Pando/Raybert (Produced by Peter Fonda), 1969
Screenplay by Peter Fonda, Dennis Hopper, and Terry
Southern
Directed by Dennis Hopper

Time: 1969
Place: On the southern route from California to Louisiana
Two men in their twenties, Billy and Wyatt, take to the road on their motorcycles. After a quick stop across the Mexican border to buy drugs, they set off across the Southwest and Texas, heading for the Mardi Gras in New Orleans.

In a small Texas town, Billy and Wyatt land in jail on a minor charge. There they meet George Hanson, a local man also in his twenties, from a good family. An ex-jock, George is now a lawyer for the local ACLU and a budding alcoholic. He has been put in jail overnight to sober up. George has been through this before and is on good terms with the local police. He gets Billy and Wyatt out of jail the next morning, and they invite George to travel with them. Donning his football helmet for protection, George climbs aboard.

· That night, around a camp fire, Billy and Wyatt offer George some marijuana, which he smokes for the first time. Staring up at the starry sky, they see a flash of light, and George gives his interpretation.

GEORGE
(exhales)

That was a UFO, beamin' back at ya. Me and Eric Heisman was down in Mexico two weeks ago—we seen forty of 'em flying in formation. They—they—they've got bases all over the world now, you know. They've been coming here ever since nineteen forty-six—when the scientists first started bouncing radar beams off the moon. And they have been livin' and workin' among us in vast quantities ever since. The government knows all about 'em.

[BILLY
What are you talkin', man?]

GEORGE

Mmmmm—well, you just seen one of 'em, didn't ya? They are people, just like us—from within our own solar system. Except that their society is more highly evolved. I mean, they don't have no wars, they got no monetary system, they don't have any leaders, because, I mean, each man is a leader. I mean, each man—because of their technology, they are able to feed, clothe, house and transport themselves equally—and with no effort. Why don't they reveal themselves to us is because if they did it would cause a general panic. Now, I mean, we still have leaders upon whom we rely for the release of this information. These leaders have decided to repress this information because of the tremendous shock that it would cause to our antiquated systems. Now, the result of this has been that the Venutians have contacted people in all walks of life—all walks of life—

(laughs)

Yes. It—it—it would be a devastating blow to our anti-quated system—so now the Venutians are meeting with people in all walks of life—in an advisory capacity. For once man will have a god-like control over his own destiny. He will have a chance to transcend and to evolve with some equality for all.

Last Summer

An Alsid Francis Production
(Produced by Alfred Crown and Sidney Beckerman), 1969
Screenplay by Eleanor Perry
Based on the novel by Evan Hunter
Directed by Frank Perry

Time: 1969
Place: Affluent beach community
Three upper-middle-class teenagers, adrift one summer at their parents' beach houses, encounter an ungainly, sensitive girl, Rhoda, also at the beach for the season. The group of three are savvy, manipulative, and curious about their new acquaintance. They see how uncomfortable Rhoda is with their faster, more sophisticated behavior but press her to become more involved in their precocious activities. One rainy afternoon the four sprawl out at one of their parents' houses, and Rhoda begins to reveal the painful story of her mother's death.

RHODA
It was a bet my mother made with this man. She bet she could swim out to the sandbar and back without stopping

to rest. Everyone was at a party at our house—there'd been a party on Friday night and another one on Saturday night and this was Sunday and I suppose they were all a little bored. I don't know exactly how it started—I was in my nightgown going around kissing everyone goodnight. They were saying that my mother was a great swimmer and one of the men said that women have an extra layer of fat around their bodies so they can stay in the water for a long time without getting chilled and my mother got mad about this extra layer of fat talk because she was very slim. I have a picture of her in my Memory Book that shows she was practically skinny. Well, my mother said she had a lot of endurance and she certainly did *not* have an extra layer of fat. Then my father said that my mother had swum to this sandbar about a half mile off shore and back without stopping and this man said that was impossible and my mother said she could do it again any time and the man said how about right now? They all smelled of whiskey when I kissed them. I remember this man who made the bet cupped my behind with both hands and kissed me goodnight right on the mouth—and then my mother took me upstairs and changed into her bathing suit. Afterwards she came into my room. Her suit was red and she was wearing a short white terry cloth robe and she looked very pretty and excited. She smelled of whiskey too but she didn't drink a lot—only enough to feel happy, she always said. She acted very happy that night and she turned out my lamp and closed the door and that was the last time I ever saw her—

Goodbye, Mr. Chips

MGM/APJAC (Produced by Arthur F. Jacobs), 1969
Screenplay by Terence Rattigan
Directed by Herb Ross

Time: 1946
Place: England
Arthur Chipping, called Mr. Chips by the boys of Brookfield Academy, has been the master of Latin for sixty years
and the headmaster for two. He is an institution at the
school, which is a bastion of English tradition, and in several
instances he has taught three generations of the same family. His ambition had always been to be headmaster. This
position eluded him, however, until shortly before the end
of World War II, when a war-related vacancy occurred. By
then he was well into his eighties and soon to retire. Following is his farewell speech to the boys of Brookfield.

———

CHIPS

Unhappily, I have two more names to add to the Brookfield
roll of honor, both men killed in the last few days of the
German War. The first is a Wing-Commander, Charles William Dickerson-Brown, killed over Berlin. A most generous-
minded and highly promising boy whose future I predicted
a great success. The second is Ober Lieutenant Max Staetel—
(pause)
Max Staetel was our German master here for twenty years,
and he was a great personal friend of mine. That, of course,
is unimportant. But he was a gentle and kind-hearted man
who loved Brookfield and England very much. He will be
very much missed. Not least by me. And now before passing
to events of the coming school week, I hope you'll forgive

me if I make an announcement regarding myself. This is
the last time I shall be addressing you as headmaster. Like
so many others, my services have come to an end with the
war, and next term you will have another headmaster. I,
myself, will be leaving Brookfield for good. I thank the boy
who said "shame," but if it was the boy I think it was—
Farley, T. F., I must tell you he is by nature a little prone
to exaggerate. I may remind him that I once had occasion
to reprimand him for exaggeration. I gave him one mark
for an exercise and he exaggerated it into a seven.

(pause)

Well, well, I thank you all then, but I beg to remind you
that I haven't really been a headmaster at all. Just "acting,"
"temporary," "on probation." Oh yes, I know my portrait's
up there with the others— But it's an awful fraud—and
quite a puzzle for posterity. "How did it ever get up there?"
they'll ask. Well, it jolly well needed a world war to do it,
I could tell them.

(pause)

Anyway, that war is over and now we may have to face the
future, you and I. I know mine, but I don't know yours.
You're growing up into a new world—a very exciting one,
perhaps—but, for sure, a very changed world. It may even
be a place that has no place for Brookfield—at least not the
Brookfield I have known for so many years, and you still
know now. Well, if such changes do come to our school,
you must accept them without rancor or bitterness. As for
me, well, I won't have to accept any changes at all, will I.
Because Brookfield for me will be only memories, and they
can't change an old chap's memories, however hard they
try. They are memories I shall always cherish, and for which
I am now most deeply and truly grateful. Just one more
thing. I'm not leaving Brookfield altogether. I'm taking
rooms in the town.

(pause)

Thank you. Well, when you come to see me in the after years, as I hope some of you will, and you're all very grand and grown up, I may well not recognize you. And you'll say: "Poor old boy, his memory's gone." But, you see, I will remember you all perfectly well, because I'll remember you as you are now. That's the point. In my mind you never grow up at all. I get older and so do all of them.

(He points to the masters behind him.)

But you always stay the same, and you always will, and in that I shall find great comfort in days to come. So you see, this isn't really goodbye at all. Simply au revoir.

Five Easy Pieces

Columbia Pictures (Produced by Bert Schneider), 1970
Screenplay by Adrien Joyce
Directed by Bob Rafelson

Time: 1970
Place: Puget Sound, Washington—a house on an island
Bobby Dupea, a young oil-rig worker, has dropped most of his ties with his music-loving family. Bobby was a serious pianist, but he's since bucked the family's expectations and taken off on the road.

Bobby travels back to his family's comfortable summer house on an island in the Pacific Northwest to see his father, who is gravely ill. In tow is Bobby's current fling, Rayette, a waitress whom Bobby stows in a motel on the mainland before going across the sound to meet his family.

Cultivated and surrounded by books and musical instruments, Bobby's family looks askance at his way of life and rebellious behavior. Bobby's sister demands that he talk to their father, who is paralyzed by a stroke, confined to a wheelchair, and unable to speak. Bobby obliges and, having wheeled his father out to a windblown field, finally attempts to communicate.

BOBBY

I don't know if you'd be particularly interested in hearing anything about me, my life. Most of it doesn't add up to much that I could relate as a way of life that you'd approve of. I move around a lot. Not because I'm looking for anything really, but 'cause I'm getting away from things that get bad if I stay. Auspicious beginnings, you know what I mean?

(pause)

I'm trying to imagine your half of this conversation. My feeling is, I don't know, that if you could talk we wouldn't be talking. It's pretty much the way that it got to be before I left. Are you all right? I don't know what to say.

(breaks down, crying)

Kate has suggested that we try to, but I don't know . . . I think that she feels that we've got some understanding to reach. She totally denies the fact that we weren't ever that comfortable with one another to begin with.

(pause)

The best that I can do is apologize. But we both know that I was never really that good at it anyway.

(pause)

Sorry it didn't work out.

Klute

Warner Brothers (Produced by Alan J. Pakula), 1971
Screenplay by Andy K. Lewis and Dave Lewis
Directed by Alan J. Pakula

Time: 1971
Place: New York City
Bree Daniels wants to be a serious actress, but she is making
her living as a high-priced call girl. While Bree has pros-
pered as a call girl, she still wants to find a way of giving
up the life. She realizes that a prostitute's life, even at
Bree's classy, businesslike level of operation, is full of dangers—psychological, emotional, and physical. Bree, early
in the film, talks to her psychiatrist.

———

BREE DANIELS

All right. Loneliness. Well—separated. From other people. Forgotten. Well, as if I can be here, I can go through
the motions, right? But the truth is, I don't belong. Well,
it's more than loneliness. Hate. People hating me—and
watching me and following me and wanting to hurt me—
you know. I'm all screwed up. The truth is I hate them:
they *must* hate me. All right, the money. All right, not the
money. A kind of put-on. It gets things back together. Well,
let's say I go to one of those cattle calls, a tryout. I mean
before—before I got this job—and they'd always say thank
you very much and I'd feel, you know, brought down. They
didn't want me. Well, you have a choice, You can either
feel lonely—you know, the hate—or— So you take a call
and you go to a hotel room and there's some John you've
never seen before, but he wants you. He must, he's paying
for it. And usually they're nervous and that's all right too,
because *you're* not; you know this thing. And then for a

while, boy, they really pay attention, you're all there is. And it's not real and you don't even like them—you can even hate them, it's all right, it's safe—you know?

Who Is Harry Kellerman and Why Is He Saying Those Terrible Things About Me?

Cinema Center (Produced by Ulu Grosbard
and Herb Gardner), 1971
Screenplay by Herb Gardner
Directed by Ulu Grosbard

Time: 1971
Place: New York City
Linda is an aspiring singer/actress who, at the age of thirty-four, has not made it. She's auditioning for a new musical entitled *Now*. Present at the audition are Peter Halloran, the director; George Solloway, the famous composer/lyricist; and Sid Gill, George's collaborator.

At the audition Linda sings for Peter, George, and Sid in a voice that is, in the words of the screenwriter, "quiet and lovely and theatrically hopeless." While she sings, Sid makes a fast exit. When she's finished, Peter thanks her and waits for her to leave, but she explains to him that she can't, her hand is gripping a work-lamp pole and she is rooted to the spot. Peter leaves, convinced that she's nuts, and Linda is left alone with George. (*Note:* The following monologue does not include George's brief reply to Linda.)

LINDA (*ALLISON*)
I can't leave. I'm sorry. I can't leave.

*(She remains frozen on the chair; one hand
gripping the briefcase, the other hand gripping
the work-lamp pole; transfixed.)*

I can't seem to let go of this lamp right now. You fellas go
ahead. I'll be all right soon . . . I feel like I just auditioned
for the part of human being, and I didn't get the job. See,
it took me three weeks to get this audition and I bought a
new dress and I worked on my song and I had my hair
done by Mr. Max at $22.50, a work of art, with lashes . . . and
now I can't just leave right away . . . I can't just leave right
away. I will just have to hang around here for a while, see?
Thank you, but I can't move anyway; my hand is stuck. . . .
It happens all the time, I get stuck onto things. Chairs,
coffee cups, doorknobs, people. I'll be all right soon. Just
don't shake hands with me or anything. You have kind eyes.
It's funny to see your face after all that darkness. A nervous
face, but kind eyes. Oh, God, I hate these auditions. I'm
not what you're looking for.

(laughs)

I'm not even Linda Kaiser. She's my roommate. My name
is Allison Densmore. I never use it because it sounds so
old . . . centuries old . . . Sounds like a lot of doilies . . .
It's very beautiful here now, with the lights on. This is . . .
This is a great set for *Lucia di Lammermoor*. Dawn on the
moors. I study opera. Every day, an hour. You like opera?

(lifts her briefcase)

I've got 'em all in here. Opera is the best. People live at
the top of their lives, and die very beautifully. Lucia and
Edgardo, they meet on this moor at dawn. She saves him,
in a way, but mostly he saves her from a wild bull, and
she's crazy about him . . . but so they save each other. . . .
Mister, listen to me. I'm still auditioning. All the time I
think I'm auditioning. I wake up in the morning and the
whole world says "Thank you very much, Miss Densmore,
that'll be enough for now."

(starts to cry)

I'm crying so odd . . . one eye at a time . . .

(shakes her head)

Mostly I'd like to get my hand off this lamp. I have to go back to work soon. I'm a Corporate Librarian. That's a file clerk. With only three good notes, you gotta back yourself up with something. You think I'll be able to get this lamp in a taxi? . . . I'm crying from the left eye now . . . It's not the audition, it's not that . . . It's my birthday. I'm thirty-four years old today. I'm not prepared. I'm prepared for twenty-two. Right now, I could do a great twenty-two. I woke up this morning, and all of a sudden I was not young. I—I was not old, but I'm all of a sudden not young. Not young enough for this dress. And not young enough to be a Corporate Librarian with three good notes and a briefcase full of grand opera. Mister, I don't understand what happened to the time. All of a sudden I'm going into my tenth year of looking for a new apartment. I'm not much of a singer, and I'm not a gifted file clerk, either. The one thing I'm good at is . . . being married. But my husband wasn't. That was ten years ago.

(laughs)

I've never learned another trade. The time, mister. It's not a thief at all like they say. It's something much sneakier. It's an embezzler, up nights, juggling the books so you don't notice anything's missing. . . . Hey, I let go of the lamp.

Last Tango in Paris

Les Artistes Associes/PEA/UA
(Produced by Alberto Grimaldi), 1972
Screenplay by Bernardo Bertolucci and Franco Arcalli
Directed by Bernardo Bertolucci

Time: 1973

Place: Paris

Paul is an American in his forties, living in Paris. A former journalist, he is adrift without work. He lives alone immediately following the bloody suicide of his French wife, who ran a seedy pension. Angry and directionless, Paul meets a young woman, Jeanne, just twenty, as they both look over the same vacant apartment. She is the daughter of a respectable middle-class couple. She is engaged to be married to a young man who's happily obsessed with cinéma verité films and follows her around with a movie camera, lovingly recording her every mood and movement.

Paul and Jeanne are drawn to each other. Paul rents the apartment. They meet there periodically and enjoy erotic experiences. He insists that they remain anonymous—no names, no knowledge of their lives outside the apartment. They fall in love, but he more obsessively than she. Jeanne eventually tries to break her addiction to Paul.

In this monologue, during an earlier, quiet moment at the apartment, Paul does talk about his past.

PAUL

My father was a . . . a drunk, whore-fucker, bar fighter, supermasculine, and he was tough . . . My mother was . . . very poetic, also drunk, and my memories 'bout when I was a kid was of her being arrested nude. We lived in a small town. Farming community. We lived on a farm. Well,

I'd come home after school and she'd be gone on a—in jail or something. I used to have to milk a cow. Every morning and every night. And I liked that, but I remember one time I was all dressed up to go out and take this girl to a basketball game. And I started to go out and my father said, "You have to milk the cow." And I asked him, "Would you please milk it for me?" And he said, "No, get your ass out there!" So I went out, and I was in a hurry and didn't have time to change my shoes, and I had cowshit all over my shoes, and on the way to the basketball game it smelled in the car. I don't know . . . Just . . . I—I can't remember very many good things. One. Maybe . . . There was a farmer, a very nice guy. Old guy, very poor and worked real hard, and I used to work in a ditch draining land for farming, and he wore overalls, and he smoked a clay pipe, and half the time he wouldn't put tobacco in it . . . he hated work. It was hot and dirty, and I broke my back. I'd watch the spit which would run down the pipe stem and hang on the bowl of the pipe. And I used to make bets with myself on when it was going to fall off, and I always lost. Never saw it fall off. I'd just look around, and it'd be gone, and then the new one would be there. And then we had a beautiful . . .
My mother taught me to love nature. I guess that was the most she could do. We had in front of the house . . . we had this big field, meadow . . . it was a mustard field in the summer, and we had a big black dog named Dutchy, and she used to hunt for rabbits in that field. But she couldn't see them, and so she'd have to leap up in this mustard field, look around very quickly to see where the rabbits were, and it was very beautiful even if she never caught the rabbits.

Paper Moon

Paramount/Saticoy (Produced by Peter Bogdanovich), 1973
Screenplay by Alvin Sargent
Based on the novel *Addie Pray,* by Joe David Brown
Directed by Peter Bogdanovich

Time: 1936, the Depression
Place: Rural Kansas and Missouri
Moses Pray, a good-hearted con artist in his late twenties,
and Addie Loggins, a ten-year-old girl who may or may not be
Moses's daughter, are "partners in crime." As they crisscross
the back roads and small towns of the rural Midwest, often
in stolen cars, they run cons together, swindling unsuspecting country folk and storekeepers out of their scarce dollars.

Their tempers flare occasionally, but they've developed
a solid relationship. They depend on and respect each other.

Moses, however, takes up with a Miss Trixie Delight, in
her late twenties, a dancer of sorts at carnivals and a woman
of leisure who, it's implied, keeps company with men for money and other "gifts." Down on her luck, she still travels with
her lady's maid, Imogene. While she has obviously weathered
some hard knocks, Trixie keeps her high heels clicking and
her sense of fun: She knows the fun ends as quickly as it starts.

At this point Moses has just invited Trixie and Imogene to
travel with him and Addie. Along the road they make a rest
stop in the middle of fields and rolling hills. After lunch Addie
goes up a hill and refuses to rejoin the group at the car. Trixie
finally tromps up the hill to try to get Addie, who's obviously
jealous of the additional travelers, to come down to the car.

TRIXIE

Hey, what's up, kiddo? Daddy says you're wearin' a sad
face. Ain't good to have a sad face. Hey! Hey, how would

you like a colorin' book? Would you like that? You like
Mickey the Mouse?

stunned but (*little girl kicks her*)
light
Ohhh—son-of-a-bitch! Woo . . . Ah, now come on down
to the car and let's all be friends. You see me smile? Come
on, let's see you smile like Aunt Trixie. Now, come on,
come on down to the car with Mademoiselle.

(*pause*)

Kiddo, I understand how you feel, but you don't have to
worry. One of these days you're gonna be just as pretty as
Mademoiselle, maybe prettier. You already got bone structure. When I was your age, I didn't have no bone structure.
Took me years to get bone structure. And don't think bone
structure's not important. Nobody started to call me Mademoiselle until I was seventeen and gettin' a little bone
structure. When I was your age, I was skinnier than a pole.
I never thought I'd have nothin' up here. It's gonna happen
up there too.

(*pause*)

getting
provoked
Look, I'll tell you what—want me to show you how to use
cosmetics? Look, I'll let you put on my earrings—you're
gonna see how pretty you're gonna be. And I'll show you
how to make up your eyes, and your lips. And I'll see to it
you get a little bra or somethin'. But right now you're gonna
pick your little ass up, you're gonna drop it in the back seat,
and you're gonna cut out the crap, you understand?

(*pause*)

more provoked
You're gonna ruin it, ain't ya? Look, I don't wanna wipe
you out, and I don't want you wipin' me out, ya know? So
I'm gonna level with ya, okay? Now, you see, with me it's
just a matter of time. I don't know why, but somehow I
just don't manage to hold on real long. So, if you wait it
out a little it'll be over, ya know? Even if I want a fellow,
somehow I always manage to get it screwed up. Maybe I'll
get a new pair of shoes, a nice dress, a few laughs . . .

Times are hard . . . Now, if you fool around on the hill
up here, then you don't get nothin', I don't get nothin', he
don't get nothin'. So, how about it, honey? Just for a little
while. Let old Trixie sit up front with her big tits.

The Way We Were

Columbia/Rastar (Produced by Ray Stark), 1973
Screenplay by Arthur Laurents
Directed by Sydney Pollack

Time: 1940s
Place: New York City
Katie Morosky and Hubbell Gardner begin as college ac-
quaintances in the late 1930s. She, a Jewish girl from New
York City, is an energetic activist, committed to the current
leftist movements. He, a good looking WASP, is a popular
athlete and aspiring writer.

Years after graduation they meet again at a nightclub in
New York City. By now Katie has lost some of her former
awkwardness and has blossomed into a self-possessed young
woman. The tentative attraction they felt for each other in
college turns into real love and, although opposites, they
become a couple.

While very much in love, their personalities are frequently at odds. Late one night Hubbell comes by the radio
station where Katie works and tells her he doesn't think
their relationship can work, that their styles clash. He
returns the key to her apartment and leaves. That night
Katie calls him where he is staying, at his friend J. J.'s apartment.

KATIE

Honey? . . . Hubbell? . . . Wait a minute . . . hold on a
minute. Don't go away. Listen, Hubbell, um, this is kind
of peculiar. I know that I don't have to apologize for what
I said, because I know that you know and, um, but I often
know that you, I mean, you know that I don't feel exactly
"bright eyed and bushy tailed" as J. J. would say. Uh . . .
anyway, the peculiar thing is, I, uh . . . it's really a request,
you know, a favor. Uh . . . you see I can't sleep, Hubbell,
and it would help me so much if you could, well, if I had
someone to talk to. You know, if I had a best friend or
something to talk about it with. Only you're my best friend.
Isn't that dumb? I'm dumb. You're the best friend I ever
had. And . . . it would help me so much if you could just
come over and you'd see me for a time. Listen . . . Hubbell,
I promise I won't touch you or . . . beg you . . . or em-
barrass you. You see, I have to talk to my best friend about
someone we both know. So could . . . Hubbell, could you
please come over right away, please?

The Conversation

Paramount/Francis Ford Coppola, 1974
Screenplay by Francis Ford Coppola
Directed by Francis Ford Coppola

Time: 1974
Place: San Francisco
Harry Caul is a mild-mannered, middle-aged electronic
surveillance professional, the tops in his field. Unmarried,
Harry lives alone in a supposedly bug-proof apartment. He

reveals little about himself even to his lover, a woman whom he sees only occasionally.

On assignment, Harry overhears a young executive, Mark, and a young woman, Ann, discussing what sounds like plans for a murder. Later, in his workshop, he listens over and over again to the tape of their conversation, becoming obsessed with the young woman's voice. He wonders if he should try to stop this intended killing and, if so, how.

He is drawn more deeply into the case, and one foggy evening in a San Francisco park he finds and follows Ann. They do not talk to each other. However, Harry begins to speak in Ann's direction.

HARRY

My name is Harry Caul. I live here in the city, in an apartment building that I own. 220 Polk Street.
> *(suddenly)*

Can you hear me? Are you listening?
> *(There is no reaction from her; she keeps*
> *walking, slowly.)*

I would tell you more about myself . . . but there's so little. I . . . never did well. When I was younger, I never did well at school. My father wanted me to be a printer, so he'd be sure I could make a living. He went to college, and he was very disappointed in me.
> *(She doesn't look at him; fog is blowing across*
> *levels of the park.)*

My mother was a Roman Catholic . . .
> *(almost passionately telling her these things)*

I was very sick when I was a boy. I was paralyzed in my left arm and my left leg, and couldn't walk for six months. I remember . . . when one doctor told me that I'd never be able to walk again.

*(The fog momentarily causes her to disappear,
then come back.)*

My mother used to lower me into a hot bath . . . it was therapy. Once the doorbell rang, and she left me propped on the tub, while she answered it. I could hear her talking downstairs while I began to slip into the water . . . I felt the water up to my chin, and my mouth, and my nose . . . and then my eyes. I remember I could see under the water. But I couldn't lift myself out of it. I remember I wasn't afraid. When I woke up later, my skin was greasy from the holy oil she had rubbed on my body . . . And I remember being disappointed that I had survived.

(view on ANN—faintly there)

I like to eat . . . but I've never liked potatoes . . .

(view on HARRY moving)

When I was five years old I was introduced to a friend of my father's and for no reason at all, I hit him with all my strength in his stomach. He died a year later.

(He sits on a small bench in the path.)

He had an ulcer . . . But my father always said he had died partly because of me. My mother said he would have died anyway. When I was four I took a puppy I loved and hit it over the head with a toy hammer. I hated a nun because she slapped me . . . but I loved the Virgin Mary because she gave me anything I wanted when I prayed to her. On my thirty-sixth birthday, as a birthday present to myself, I turned in a false alarm. And I remember a girl named Marjorie who kissed me on the lips and told me she loved me on the day her family was moving back to Virginia because her father was an officer in the Navy.

*(ANN is standing, disappearing . . . now
gone.)*

I am miserly and cheap, a penny pinching . . . I enjoy looking at my face in the mirror. I am not afraid of death . . . but I am afraid of murder.

*(Silence; HARRY looks up to the second terrace
of the park; it is covered with fog.)*

Are you there?

*(Full view of HARRY, sitting alone on the
bench)*

Scenes from a Marriage

A Cinematograph AB Production
(Produced by Lars-Owe Carlberg), 1974
Screenplay by Ingmar Bergman
Directed by Ingmar Bergman

Time: 1973
Place: Swedish city

After ten years of marriage and two children (young girls),
Marianne and Johan, both in their late thirties, separate
and divorce. Johan is a professor at a university. Marianne
is a lawyer—divorce and family matters are her specialty.

While their marriage had seemed a model of stability
and mutual trust, Johan announced unexpectedly to Marianne that he was having a love affair with another woman
and was going to leave Marianne and the children to live
with her.

After the initial agony of separation they begin to rebuild
their lives. They continue to see each other at various in-
tervals and try to understand their continuing need for one
another.

At this meeting Marianne is feeling confident and strong.
She has a new lover. Johan is having troubles—mostly
professional but also with his love life. They have met at
Marianne's house to have dinner, and they are talking over
drinks.

Marianne chides Johan for not doing his part—financially and in other ways—for the children. Johan is critical about the children, with whom he's had trouble communicating. Johan says, bluntly, "Children grow up, relations are broken off . . . love gives out." Marianne says she thinks she and Johan were spoiled and have squandered their lives, becoming bitter and bored. She wants to know what went wrong and, remembering the fun the family used to have, how they became bored. Johan responds.

———

JOHAN

I'll tell you something banal. We're emotional illiterates. And not only you and I—practically everybody, that's the depressing thing. We're taught everything about the body and about agriculture in Madagascar and about the square root of pi, or whatever the hell it's called, but not a word about the soul. We're abysmally ignorant, about both ourselves and others. There's a lot of loose talk nowadays to the effect that children should be brought up to know all about brotherhood and understanding and coexistence and equality and everything else that's all the rage just now. But it doesn't dawn on anyone that we must first learn something about ourselves and our own feelings. Our own fear and loneliness and anger. We're left without a chance, ignorant and remorseful among the ruins of our ambitions. To make a child aware of its soul is something almost indecent. You're regarded as a dirty old man. How can you ever understand other people if you don't know anything about yourself? Now you're yawning, so that's the end of the lecture. I had nothing more to say anyway. Some more brandy? Then we'll decide what to do about supper.

Harry and Tonto

Twentieth Century-Fox (Produced by Paul Mazursky), 1974
Screenplay by Paul Mazursky and Josh Greenfield
Directed by Paul Mazursky

Time: 1974

Place: New York City

Harry, a widowed, retired teacher in his seventies, has lived in his New York City apartment, with his cat Tonto, for many years. He has recently learned that the city authorities want to tear his building down to make a parking lot.

One afternoon, walking home from the local store with a bag of groceries in one hand and Tonto's leash in the other, Harry is stopped by a young kid who asks if he has some spare change. Harry says he's got some change but none to spare and would the kid like a banana? Suddenly the boy knocks Harry's groceries out of his hands and runs away.

Harry returns home. As he is putting the groceries away, he talks to Tonto.

———

HARRY

Would you believe it, Tonto? Mugged four times in one year . . . In a way, I'm glad Anne isn't alive to see it. She loved this neighborhood. And who could argue with her. It was like living in Shakespeare's London. Bristling with energy. It's still bristling, but with the energy gone . . . There were trolleys, Tonto! Cobblestones! The aroma of corned beef and cabbage spiced with zesty apple strudel . . . You had to hand-crank the cars. Reos. Hudsons. Franklins.

(petting the cat, who is falling asleep)

Those were names fit for a car. These days a man doesn't know if he's driving a car or an animal. Mustang, Jaguar, Cougar, Pinto . . . Silly! . . . My first car was a Hudson . . . Hendrik Hudson . . . They should only name cars after explorers and rivers . . . I'd love to drive a Mississippi . . . or an Amazon . . . a convertible Rio Grande . . . or an automatic Thames. A stickshift Yangtse . . . I used to drive Burt around on his paper route . . . Oh, we had paper routes in those days . . . Get up really early and help the boy make his pocket money . . . This was a fine neighborhood . . .

(yawns)

Run-down . . . running down . . . it all runs down sooner or later . . . where else could I live? I still know a lot of people around here, Tonto. A lot of people. You know people, that's home . . .

Dog Day Afternoon

Warners/ACC (Produced by Martin Bregman
and Martin Elfland), 1975
Screenplay by Frank Pierson
Based on the book by Patrick Mann
Directed by Sidney Lumet

Time: August 22, 1972
Place: Brooklyn
This film is based on an actual, botched attempt to rob a bank in Brooklyn. Confronted by police, the two doomed robbers, Sonny and Sal, seize the bank employees as hostages. Crowds and TV camera crews gather outside on a

hot August afternoon to watch and become part of the explosive spectacle.

Sonny, married, in his twenties and the father of two boys, is from a working class section of Flatbush. He's trying to make a quick score to get money for a sex-change operation for his male lover, Leon.

Monologue One. Heidi, Sonny's wife, talks to the police about Sonny, as the hostage situation builds.

Monologue Two. Sonny reads a statement for the cameras and crowd, as he realizes the odds of his surviving the standoff are against him.

Monologue One

HEIDI

The transistor goes Sonny *what?* I couldn't believe my ears, so I shut the transistor, get outta here, who needs this? I say Sonny didn't do it. It's not him to rob a bank. It's not him to hurt anybody, to threaten anybody, to steal or do anything wrong. 'Cause he's never done nothin' wrong from the day I know him. . . . Only he tells me this and he tells me that, he's with the Mafia, I say, Sonny, where do you get this money, you're on welfare, how can you rent a new Eldorado, red, you don't like the color you rent a yellow. So night before last we're at Coney Island, he's on the rides with the kids, an' I have this habit of goin' in glove compartments an' all, an' I see this gun with bullets in there, an' I go to myself, oh God, Sonny! That's all I had to see, I didn't say anything. And things are adding in my head, how crazy he's been acting, and in with a bad crowd, an' I look at him, he's yellin' at the kids like a madman. So inna car I said to him, Sonny, what you gonna do with the gun? You gonna shoot me and dump my body inna river or what? I was so scared of him, I never been scared of Sonny never. You know, his mother says the cops was always at our house, we was always fighting. I hit him with the jack of the car once, but I only missed and hit myself, you should of seen my leg. And all he would ever do is put on his coat and go out. So they say it's Sonny but I don't believe it. He might of done it, his body functions might of done it, but not he himself.

Monologue Two

SONNY

Being of sound mind and body, and all that shit . . . To my darling wife Leon whom I love as no other man has loved another man in all eternity, I leave $2,700 from my $10,000 life insurance policy, to be used for your sex change operation. If there is money left over it is to go to you on the first anniversary of my death, at my grave. I expect you to be a real woman then, and your life full of happiness and joy. To my sweet wife, Heidi, five thousand from the same policy. You are the only woman I have ever loved, and I re-pledge my love to you in this sad moment, and to little Kimmy and Jimmy. I hope you remember me, Jimmy. You are the little man of the family now, and will have to look after them for me. To my mother I ask forgiveness. You don't understand the things I did and said, but I'm me, and I'm different. I leave you the rest of the policy and my stamp collection. I want a military funeral and am entitled to one free of charge. Life and love are not easy and we have to bend a lot. I hope you find the places and the people to make you all happy as I could not. God bless you and watch over you, as I shall, until we are joined in the hereafter, sweet Leon, my Heidi, dearest Kimmy and Jimmy,

and my mother. Sonny . . . here I'll spell the last name . . .
Type that up and I'll sign it.

Next Stop, Greenwich Village

Twentieth Century-Fox (Produced by Paul Mazursky
and Tony Ray), 1975
Screenplay by Paul Mazursky
Directed by Paul Mazursky

Time: 1953
Place: Greenwich Village, New York
Larry Lapinsky leaves the Brooklyn house of his loving but
smothering parents and moves into a bare-bones Greenwich Village apartment. He's determined to make it as an
actor and gets involved with a group of struggling young
painters, actors, and writers. One evening, on deserted
Brooklyn streets, Larry cuts loose extemporaneously.

LARRY
(imitation of Dylan Thomas)
'Do not go gentle into that good night,
Old age should burn and rave at close of day;
Rage, rage against the dying of the light.
Though wise men at their end know dark is right,
Because their words had formed no lightning they
Do not go gentle into that good night.'
*(kicks a can . . . follows it, kicks it
again . . . does imitation of Brando)*
'Stella . . . Stella . . . Where are you, Stella? . . . Blanche?
What do you say, Blanche? . . . Let me tell you about the
Napoleonic Code, Blanche babe . . . '

(back to himself)

—Thank you very much, ladies and gentlemen of the Academy. This Oscar gives me great pleasure.

(He picks up the old can of soup he has been kicking, and holds it as if it is an Oscar.)

But I don't think this award goes just to Larry Lapinsky . . . No, there are a lot of other people involved in this . . . I would like to thank, first of all, my director, Elia Kazan. Without Gadge, there would be no Larry Lapinsky. It was Gadge who discovered me in the Forty-Second Street Library . . . I would like to thank the author of the film, that great Jewish writer, Eugene O'Neill . . .

(looks at the can with great emotion)

Boy, this is really something . . .

(fakes crying)

But this evening would not be complete if I didn't thank the little woman who has stood behind me all these years . . .

(looks behind him)

As a matter of fact, she's right behind me now . . . Mom, say a few words . . .

(A COP on the beat sees Larry, but Larry doesn't see the cop.)

(as Mom)

When my darling, adorable, loving son first told my husband and myself that he wanted to be an actor, I scoffed. Oh, boy, did I scoff. But, tonight, I realize that I scoffed wrongly. You don't scoff at an Academy Award winner. My son's performance as Sheriff Luke Marshall in 'Last Train to Budapest' will go down as one of the great performances in motion picture history . . . But, ladies and gentlemen of the Academy, tell me one thing, why does my son complain when I bring him a chicken to his Big-Deal Greenwich Village apartment? . . . Why? Why? Why? . . .

(quick Brando)

'I'll tell you why, Mom. Because the boy is an ingrate. He doesn't understand the Napoleonic Code . . . '

Carrie

United Artists/Redbank (Produced by Paul Monash), 1976
Screenplay by Lawrence D. Cohen
Based on the novel by Stephen King
Directed by Brian de Palma

Time: 1976
Place: Small suburban community in the Midwest
A high-school senior class misfit, Carrie White, lives alone with her mother, Margaret, who is very possibly insane. When Carrie's classmates are reprimanded for teasing her, they conspire to play a trick on her.

Suddenly, improbably, Tommy, the school's heartthrob football star, asks Carrie to be his date at the prom. Carrie is delighted and goes with him, against strong warnings from her mother.

As if in a dream, Carrie is voted "queen of the prom." At the moment of her greatest happiness a group of students triggers a rigged bucket of animal blood to spill its contents on her head, hair, and dress. She stands, uncomprehending, on the platform before the entire prom gathering. She is covered with blood. Out of her horror and humiliation Carrie, a normally sweet and unaggressive girl, unleashes violent psychokinetic powers. Standing still, frozen with shame, fear, and anger, Carrie's mind makes terrible things happen to her classmates. Fires rage and doors lock, trapping almost everyone in a bloody conflagration. Amid the screams and tears of the prom-goers, Carrie magically glides through doors that open just for her and then slam shut. She returns home. The house is filled with burning candles. Her mother, in her nightgown, is in an agitated state. Margaret White begins to talk.

MARGARET

I should have killed myself when he put it in me . . . after the first time . . . before we were married. Ralph promised never again. He promised. And I believed him. But Sin never dies. Sin never dies. At first it was all right. We lived sinlessly. We slept in the same bed but we never did. And then, that night . . . I saw him looking down at me that way. We got down on our knees to pray for strength. I smelled the whiskey on his breath and . . . he took me. *Took me!* With the stink of . . . of that filthy roadhouse whiskey on his breath, he took me . . . and *I liked it! I liked it! With all that dirty touching, oh, his hands on me, all over me!*

(breaking off, then)

I should have given you to God when you were born. But I was weak and backsliding! And now, now the devil has come home.

(sighing, then)

We'll pray.

[CARRIE
(sobbing)

Yes, Momma, *yes!*]

MARGARET
(off)

We'll pray. We'll pray. We'll pray. For the last time, we'll pray. Our Father who art in heaven . . .

[CARRIE &] MARGARET

. . . . hallowed be Thy name . . .

MARGARET
Thy kingdom come . . . thy will be done . . .

All the President's Men

Warners/Wildwood (Produced by Robert Redford
and Walter Coblenz), 1976
Screenplay by William Goldman
Based on the book by Carl Bernstein and Bob Woodward
Directed by Alan J. Pakula

Time: June 1972
Place: Washington, D.C.
This film is the story of investigative journalists Bob Woodward and Carl Bernstein, the *Washington Post* reporters who broke the news of the Watergate cover-up that led to President Richard Nixon's resignation.

In June 1972 (an election year), a group of men is arrested for breaking into the headquarters of the Democratic National Committee at the Watergate Hotel.

Woodward, an Ivy League type, relatively new at the paper, and Bernstein, a more experienced reporter, start to dig methodically and sometimes blindly into the case.

Although not particularly friendly at first, eventually they begin to trust and rely upon each other. They encounter repeated frustrations in getting Republican workers at the Committee to Reelect the President (CREEP) to tell what they know about Watergate. They drive from one address to the next, talking with fearful, uncooperative CREEP employees.

Woodward and Bernstein are in their car, parked outside the house of yet another CREEP employee on their list. The frustrations of working for a newspaper are getting to Carl. He remembers an incident early on in his career.

BERNSTEIN
(shaking his head)

My first day as a copy boy I was sixteen and wearing my only grown-up suit—it was cream colored. At two-thirty the head copy boy comes running up to me and says, "My God, haven't you washed the carbon paper yet? If it's not washed by three, it'll never be dry for tomorrow." And I said, "Am I supposed to do that?" and he said, "Absolutely, it's crucial." So I run around and grab all the carbon paper from all the desks and take it to the men's room. I'm standing there washing it and it's splashing all over me and the editor comes in to take a leak, and he says, "What the fuck do you think you're doing?" And I said, "It's two-thirty. I'm washing the carbon paper."

(BERNSTEIN looks at WOODWARD. They both get out of the car. BERNSTEIN is looking at the house.)

I'm beginning to feel like I never stopped.

(They walk toward the house.)

Network

MGM/United Artists (Produced by Howard Gottfried and Fred Caruso), 1976
Screenplay by Paddy Chayefsky
Directed by Sidney Lumet

Time: 1975
Place: New York City

Howard Beale has been the main newscaster for WUBS-TV for eleven years. He's in his early fifties, recently widowed, and childless. Due to low ratings, he's being fired,

effective in two weeks. In his first broadcast after learning
this news, Howard announces that he's going to kill himself
on the air the following Tuesday. The effect of Howard's
announcement is staggering: WUBS's ratings for his
Wednesday, Thursday, and Friday shows are phenomenal.

Meanwhile, at home, alone in bed, Howard is awakened
at 2:00 A.M., hearing a voice urging him to "go and tell the
people the truth." The voice says that he'll put the words
in Howard's mouth. When Howard asks, "Why me?" the
voice says, "Because you're on TV, dummy."

During a broadcast Howard once again sets aside the
news report and tells his viewers about the voice that contacted him. Afterward his old friend and colleague, Max
Schumacher, president of the news division, tells Howard
that he thinks Howard is having a nervous breakdown and
should go off the air. Howard responds to Max.

———

HOWARD

This is not a psychotic episode. It is a cleansing moment
of clarity.
                    (stands, an imbued man)
I am imbued, Max. I am imbued with some special spirit.
It's not a religious feeling at all. It is a choking eruption of
great electrical energy! I feel vivid and flashing as if suddenly I had been plugged into some great cosmic electro-
magnetic field. I feel connected to all living things, to flow-
ers, birds, to all the animals of the world and even to some
great unseen living force, what I think the Hindus call
prana.
            (He stands rigidly erect, his eyes staring
            mindlessly out, his face revealing the anguish
            of so transcendental a state.)
It is not a breakdown. I have never felt so orderly in my
life! It is a shattering and beautiful sensation! It is the ex-

alted flow of the space-time continuum, save that it is spaceless and timeless and of such loveliness! I feel on the verge
of some great ultimate truth.

> *(He stares haggardly at MAX, his breath*
> *coming with great difficulty now; he shouts.)*

You will not take me off the air for now or for any other
spaceless time!

> *(He promptly falls in a dead swoon onto the*
> *floor.)*

An Unmarried Woman

Twentieth Century-Fox (Produced by Paul Mazursky and Tony Ray), 1977
Screenplay by Paul Mazursky
Directed by Paul Mazursky

Time: 1977

Place: New York City

Erica is an upper-middle-class wife and mother who appears to have everything under control in her life. She has
an attentive, successful husband, Martin, and a charming,
communicative teenage daughter, Patti. Erica is pretty, she
jogs, is in good health, and has close female friends. When
Martin suddenly leaves Erica for a woman he met in Bloom-
ingdale's, Erica's life is shattered. For the first time in a
very long time she feels alone and afraid.

Monologue One. Here she talks to her psychiatrist about
her fears, past and present.

Monologue Two. Erica is on her first date with Saul, an
English painter in his mid-forties now living and working
in New York City. They are walking down the empty streets
of Soho, late at night, having deserted a party moments
before. Saul begins to tell Erica a few things about himself.

Monologue One

ERICA

I had a date with a guy and he made some comment and I said to him, it's an unfair universe . . . That's how I feel about what's happened to me. It's unfair. Why me?—And I'm afraid. I have never been afraid of anything in my life. Oh, some things. You know . . . when Patti was a baby and she had a hundred and five fever . . . I was afraid she'd die . . . I was afraid . . . I was afraid of the usual things when I was a little girl . . . But I've never really been afraid . . . Do you understand?

[TANYA

Afraid of what things?]

ERICA

Oh . . . I don't know . . . Afraid of my report card. Afraid I'd get my white pinafore dirty . . . Afraid when I got my period the first time . . .

(smiles)

—I got my period when I was thirteen. Some of my friends . . . well, not really some . . . My best friend was Karen Finestein and she got her period when she was twelve. So I figured there was something wrong with me. I had a terrible year from twelve to thirteen. Whenever I went to the bathroom I looked to see if I was getting my period yet. That's all Karen and I talked about. "Did you get it yet?" "No." Jesus . . . Then I got it. I was wearing white lace panties that my grandmother gave me for my birthday and I was sitting in my Spanish class and I suddenly felt this strange warm wetness in my crotch. And I had this weird, crazy feeling of elation. Then suddenly I was afraid . . . I was afraid of getting blood all over my white panties . . . Then the bell rang and all the kids got up and I saw Karen and I caught her eyes with mine and I

smiled and she came over and she said what are you smiling about and I said I got my period and she said "Thank
God" . . .

> *(ERICA laughs . . . TANYA doesn't . . .)*

—But what does all this have to do with anything? I don't
really see how you can help me. What can you do? You
can't live my life for me. Can you?

Monologue Two

SAUL

I have very simple tastes. I like Rembrandt, Botticelli,
Titian, Kojak, Camembert cheese, expensive shoes—I have
bad feet . . . Paris, Vermont, New York about half the
time, and being madly in love . . . I've been without the
latter for too long now.

> *(ERICA starts to laugh . . . She can't*
> *stop . . . Almost out of control . . .)*

What the hell is so funny? A man bares his soul and a
woman laughs at him.

[ERICA

You stepped in dog shit.]

> *(SAUL examines his shoe and sure enough he*
> *did . . . He begins to walk around, wiping his*
> *shoe on the ground in a comical way as he*
> *walks . . .)*

SAUL

This is the only city in the world where there is dog shit
piled on top of other dog shit . . . Future archaeologists
will learn about our civilization by examining layers of
dog do . . .

> *(drags his foot)*

I'd say this was poodle shit . . . Oh, yes, after a while you
can tell one kind from another . . . I can even tell if it's
an uptown dog or a Village dog or an East Side dog . . .

East Side dogs shit only the best . . . Village dogs shit art . . . in London, the dogs don't shit at all . . . they're not permitted to, you know . . . I've always had the theory that there's a hidden underground passage in London where all the dogs crap . . .

> *(SAUL wipes his foot and finally his shoe is
> clean . . .)*

I was born in London, you know . . . My father owned a delicatessen in Stepney Green . . . That's the Lower East Side of London . . . One day when I was six, my parents had an argument . . . My mother threw a pickled herring at Dad . . . It missed him, but splattered against the wall . . . I took one look at the herring on the wall and that's when I decided to become an abstract expressionist . . .

Annie Hall

**United Artists (Produced by Jack Rollins and
Charles H. Joffe), 1977
Screenplay by Woody Allen and Marshall Brickman
Directed by Woody Allen**

Time: 1977
Place: Manhattan
Alvy Singer grew up in a Jewish family in Brooklyn, in a house under the roller coaster at Coney Island. Now forty, he's become a successful comedian and comedy writer. He's seen on television and recognized on the street, whether he likes it or not. He's "arrived" but is still looking for greater meaning in his life. Alvy navigates with highly developed defenses and well-cultivated neuroses.

This monologue opens the film, as Alvy looks back on

what were the best and worst of times during his love affair with Annie Hall. Shown in flashbacks, Alvy's romantic encounters with women prepared him to expect the worst. But he meets and falls in love with Annie, a refreshingly eccentric WASP in her twenties, from the middle-class Midwest. Annie's left Chippewa Falls, Wisconsin—land of frigid winters and baked hams at Christmas—to be a singer in New York—land of pastrami on rye, indoor tennis, and documentaries like *The Sorrow and the Pity* playing at revival movie houses.

Alvy and Annie enchant each other, but as the relationship develops, they find themselves pulled in conflicting directions.

ALVY

There's an old joke. Uh, two elderly women are at a Catskills mountain resort, and one of 'em says: "Boy, the food at this place is really terrible." The other one says, "Yeah, I know, and such . . . small portions." Well, that's essentially how I feel about life. Full of loneliness and misery and suffering and unhappiness, and it's all over much too quickly. The—the other important joke for me is one that's uh, usually attributed to Groucho Marx, but I think it appears originally in Freud's wit and its relation to the unconscious. And it goes like this—I'm paraphrasing. Uh . . . "I would never wanna belong to any club that would have someone like me for a member." That's the key joke of my adult life in terms of my relationships with women. Tsch, you know, lately the strangest things have been going through my mind, 'cause I turned forty, tsch, and I guess I'm going through a life crisis or something, I don't know. I, uh . . . and I'm not worried about aging. I'm not one o' those characters, you know. Although I'm balding slightly on top, that's about the worst you can say about me. I, uh, I think I'm gonna get better as I get older, you know? I think I'm gonna be the—the balding virile type, you know, as opposed to say the, uh, distinguished gray, for instance, you know? 'Less I'm neither o' those two. Unless I'm one o' those guys with saliva dribbling out of his mouth who wanders into a cafeteria with a shopping bag screaming about socialism.

(sighing)

Annie and I broke up and I—I still can't get my mind around that. You know, I—I keep sifting the pieces o' the relationship through my mind and—and examining my life and tryin' to figure out where did the screw-up come, you know, and a year ago we were . . . tsch, in love. You know, and-and-and . . . And it's funny, I'm not—I'm not a morose type. I'm not a depressive character. I—I—I, uh—

(laughing)

—you know, I was a reasonably happy kid, I guess. I was brought up in Brooklyn during World War II.

The Goodbye Girl

Warners/Rastar (Produced by Ray Stark), 1977
Screenplay by Neil Simon
Directed by Herbert Ross

Time: 1977
Place: New York City
Paula, an out-of-work dancer in her thirties, and her daughter, Lucy, ten, live in an apartment in New York City. Paula's live-in boyfriend, Tony, has recently deserted them and moved to California. He sublet the apartment without Paula's knowledge. When the new subletter, Eliot Garfield, arrives, Paula reluctantly lets him live with her and Lucy.

Eliot, in his thirties, is an actor from Chicago who has moved to New York to play Richard III Off Broadway.

One evening, on her way home from dance class, Paula has her purse stolen. After dinner she explains to Eliot that she's strapped for money and gamely asks to borrow some. Eliot responds generously, offering to pay all living expenses until she gets a job. Paula, suspicious, asks him what he wants in return. When Eliot says, "Just be nice to me," Paula misinterprets his remark and tells him to go to hell. This is Eliot's response.

———

ELIOT

Will you listen very, very carefully to me? Just for once— This may be the last time I ever talk to you. Not everyone in this world is after your magnificent body, lady. In the first place, it's not so magnificent. It's fair, but it ain't keepin' me up nights, ya know? I don't even think you're very pretty. Maybe if you smiled once and awhile, okay, but I don't want you to do anything against your religion. And you are *not* the only person in this city ever to get dumped on. I myself am a recent dumpee. I am a dedicated actor, Paula, ya know? I am dedicated to my art and my craft. I value what I do. And because of a mentally arthritic director, I am about to play the second greatest role in the history of the English-speaking theater like a double order of fresh California fruit salad. When I say "nice," I mean "nice"—ya know, decent, fair. I deserve it, because I'm a nice, decent and fair person. I don't wanna jump on your bones. I don't even want to see you in the morning. But I'll tell you what I do like about you, Paula: Lucy. Lucy's your best part. Lucy is worth puttin' up with *you* for. So here is fourteen dollars for the care and feeding of that terrific kid. *You* get zippity-doo-dah. You want any money? Borrow it from your ten-year-old daughter.

(pause)

I am now going inside my room to meditate away my hostility toward you. Personally, I don't think it can be done.

Autumn Sonata

Personafilm/ITC (Produced by Ingmar Bergman), 1978
Screenplay by Ingmar Bergman
Directed by Ingmar Bergman

Time: 1978
Place: Southern Norway
Charlotte, an aging, beautiful, and worldly concert pianist, and her daughter, Eva, an unglamorous, sensitive woman in her late thirties, reflect on what their relationship has become over the years. They are attempting to come to terms with each other.

Eva grapples with her love for her mother, whom she idolizes, as well as her feelings of rejection, jealousy, and bitterness, and her sense that Charlotte's accomplished life had little room for her.

Eva, after college, was engaged to a doctor and lived with him for several years. She wrote two books, contracted tuberculosis, and broke off her engagement. She moved from Oslo to a small town in the south of Norway and began working as a journalist. She is married to Viktor, a parson. Their child died accidentally—drowned in an old well on their property—before his fourth birthday.

Charlotte visits Eva and Viktor at their home, where Charlotte's self-involved devotion to her art lifts momentarily as she listens to Eva, who tries to explain what it has been like being her daughter.

EVA

To you I was a doll that you played with when you had time. If I was sick or naughty, you handed me over to the nanny or to Father. You shut yourself in and worked, and no one was allowed to disturb you. I used to stand outside the door listening. When you stopped for coffee, I'd steal in to see if you really did exist. You were kind, but your mind was elsewhere. If I asked you anything, you hardly answered. I'd sit on the floor looking at you. You were tall and beautiful, the room was cool and airy, the awnings were lowered. Outside a breeze stirred the leaves and everything was swathed in an unreal green light. Sometimes you'd let me row you out on the inlet. You had a long, white, low-cut summer dress which showed your breasts. They were so beautiful. You were barefoot and had plaited your hair in a thick braid. You liked to look down into the water. It was clear and cold, and you could see the big stones far down on the bottom, the plants and the fish. Your hair got wet and your hands too. Because you always looked so nice, I wanted to be nice too. I grew meticulous with my clothing. I was always anxious that you wouldn't like my appearance. I thought I was so ugly, you see, lean and angular with big cow's eyes and big ugly lips and no eyebrows or lashes; and my arms were far too long and my feet were too big and my toes too flat and . . . no, I thought I looked almost repulsive. But you hardly ever showed that you were worried over my appearance. Once you said: "You should have been a boy," and then you laughed so that I wouldn't be upset. I was, of course. I cried for a whole week in secret, because you detested tears—other people's tears.

Then suddenly one day your suitcases would be standing downstairs and you'd be talking on the phone in a foreign language. I used to go into the nursery and pray to God that something would happen to stop you from going, that Grandma would die or that there'd be an earthquake or that all the airplanes would have engine trouble. But you always went. All the doors were open and the wind blew through the house and everyone talked at once, and you came up to me and put your arms around me and kissed me and hugged me and kissed me again and looked at me and smiled at me and you smelled nice but strange and you yourself were a stranger. You were already on the way, you didn't see me. I used to think: Now my heart will stop, I'm dying, it hurts so much, I'll never be happy again. Only five minutes have passed, how can I bear such pain for two months? And I cried in Father's lap, and he sat quite still with his soft little hand on my head. He went on and on sitting there, smoking his old pipe, puffing away till the smoke was all around us. Sometimes he'd say something: "Let's go to a movie this evening," or "What about ice cream for dinner today?" But I couldn't have cared less about movies or ice cream because I was dying. So the days and the weeks passed. Father and I shared the loneliness quite well. We hadn't much to say to each other, but it was so peaceful with him, and I never disturbed him. Sometimes he looked rather worried. I didn't know he was always short of money, but whenever I came clumping along his face would brighten and we'd have a talk or he'd just pat me with his pale little hand. Or else he'd be sitting on the leather sofa with Uncle Otto, drinking a brandy, and both of them mumbling to each other. I wonder if they heard what they said. Or else Uncle Harry was there, and when they played chess it was extra quiet. I could hear three different clocks ticking in the house. Several days before you were due home I'd get feverish with excitement, and at the same time I was worried in case I got really ill because I knew you were afraid of sick people.

And then when you did come I could hardly bear it, I was so happy, and I couldn't say anything either, so sometimes you were impatient and said: "Eva doesn't seem to be very pleased to have her mother at home again." Then my cheeks flamed and I broke out in a sweat but couldn't say anything—I hadn't any words because you had taken charge of all the words at home. I loved you, it was a matter of life and death—I thought so anyway—but I distrusted your words. I knew instinctively that you hardly ever meant what you said. You have such a beautiful voice, Mother. When I was little I could feel it all over my body when you spoke to me, and often you were cross with me for not hearing what you said. It was because I was listening to your voice, but also because I didn't understand what you said. I didn't understand your words—they didn't match your intonation or the expression in your eyes. The worst of all was that you smiled when you were angry. When you hated Father you called him "my dearest friend," when you were tired of me you said: "darling little girl." Nothing fitted. No, wait, Mother, I must finish speaking. I know I'm tipsy, but if I hadn't had a drink I wouldn't have said what I have. Later, when my courage fails and I don't dare to say any more, or keep quiet because I'm ashamed of what I've said, you can talk and explain, and I'll listen and understand, just as I've always listened and understood. In spite of everything, it wasn't so bad being your little child. There was nothing wrong in my loving you. You tolerated me pretty well, as you had your travels. But one thing I've never understood is your relationship to Father. I've thought of you both so much lately, but your life together is a riddle. Sometimes I think you were totally dependent on Father, although he was so much weaker than you were. In some way you were considerate to him, as you never were to me and Helena. You spoiled him and talked of him as if he were made of finer material. Yet poor Father was very mediocre really—kind of meek and unoffending. I gathered you paid Father's debts on several occasions. Wasn't that so?

Interiors

United Artists/A Jack Rollins– Charles H. Joffe Production, 1978
Screenplay by Woody Allen
Directed by Woody Allen

Time: 1978
Place: Tasteful Long Island beach house and New York City
Interiors explores the life of an upper-middle-class family with three grown daughters.

Arthur and Eve have raised three bright, creative women: Flyn, a working actress; Renata, a published poet; and Joey, who is struggling to carve out a career for herself. She has been unable to make it as an actress or artist and intends to try her hand at writing now. Joey lives with Mike, a filmmaker. Competition, jealousies, shifting family alliances, and a yearning for improved connection with each other punctuate their relationships.

Eve, formerly a successful interior decorator, has been, and still is, prone to serious emotional instability and breakdowns. She is emotionally remote from her family.

Arthur, a lawyer, eventually divorces Eve and marries Pearl, a warm, good-hearted widow, in a ceremony at the family beach house. That night, after the wedding, with everyone asleep, Joey thinks she hears her mother outside the house and starts speaking to her.

JOEY

Mother? Is that you?

> *(sighing, after a pause)*

You shouldn't be here. Not tonight. I'll take you home.

> *(EVE stands, her face in shadow, behind the*
> *door; she looks into the living room while*
> *JOEY continues to talk.)*

You look so strange and tired. I feel like we're in a dream together.

> *(JOEY walks to a straight-backed chair, near*
> *the fireplace, and sits down.)*

Please don't look so sad. It makes me feel so guilty.

> *(sighing)*

I'm so consumed with guilt. It's ironic . . . because, uh, I care for you so . . . and you have nothing but disdain for me.

> *(JOEY takes a sip of her drink. Her mother,*
> *now in the living room, stands by a window,*
> *leaning her head against the pane; her face is*
> *still in shadow.)*

And yet I feel guilty. I think you're, uh . . . really too perfect . . . to live in this world. I mean, all the beautifully furnished rooms, carefully designed interiors . . . everything so controlled. There wasn't any room for—uh eh, any real feelings. None. I . . . uh, between any of us. Except Renata . . . who never gave you the time of day. You worship Renata.

> *(EVE, reacting, looks intently at JOEY, her*
> *face still in shadow.)*

You worship talent. Well, what happens to those of us who can't create? What do we do? What do *I* do . . . when I'm overwhelmed with feelings about life? How do I get them out? I feel such rage toward you! Come on, Mother—don't

you see? You're not just a sick woman. That would be too
easy. The truth is . . . there's been perverseness—and
willfulness of attitude—in many of the things you've done.
At the center of—of a sick psyche, there is a sick spirit.
But I love you. And we have no other choice but to forgive
each other.

(She looks down, her speech finished. PEARL,
wearing a robe, enters the room.)

Kramer vs. Kramer

Columbia Pictures/A Stanley Jaffe Production, 1979
Screenplay by Robert Benton
Based on the novel by Avery Corman
Directed by Robert Benton

Time: 1979
Place: New York City
Ted and Joanna are a young couple in their thirties who
live in a comfortable building on the Upper East Side with
their six-year-old son, Billy. Ted is a successful advertising
executive, and Joanna does not work outside the home.
Without warning Joanna leaves Ted and Billy and goes to
California in an effort to find an identity apart from her
roles as wife and mother. Ted is left solely responsible for
Billy. This causes some drastic changes in his life. Caring
for Billy has even taken priority over his job. The result is
that Ted is fired.

Joanna returns to New York, asking for a divorce and
custody of Billy. Ted is deeply attached and committed
to his son and wants legal custody. In an effort to prove himself a worthy father, he furiously scrambles to land a
job and eventually accepts a position for which he is over-

qualified. Shortly thereafter a painful custody trial ensues.

Monologue One. At the trial Ted takes the stand.

Monologue Two. Joanna has been awarded custody of Billy. Ted has prepared Billy to go with his mother, and they are both waiting for her to arrive. When Joanna buzzes the apartment from the lobby, she asks Ted, over the intercom, to come down alone to talk to her. Ted arrives in the lobby, and she speaks.

Monologue One

TED
(speaking quietly)

When Joanna—
(to the judge, correcting himself)
—my ex-wife—when she was talking before about how unhappy she was during our marriage . . . Well, I guess most of what she said was probably true. There were a lot of things I didn't understand—a lot of things I would do different if I could. Just like I guess there are a lot of things Joanna wishes she could change . . . But we can't. Some things, once they are done, can't be undone. Joanna says she loves Billy. I believe she does. So do I. But the way it was explained to me, that's not the issue. The only thing that's supposed to matter here is what's best for Billy . . . When Joanna said why shouldn't a woman have the same ambitions as a man, I suppose she's right. But by the same token what law is it that says a woman is a better parent simply by virtue of her sex? I guess I've had to think a lot about whatever it is that makes somebody a good parent: constancy, patience, understanding . . . love. Where is it written that a man has any less of those qualities than a woman? Billy has a home with me, I've tried to make it the best I could. It's not perfect. I'm not a perfect parent.

(unconsciously echoing something Joanna said earlier)

I don't have enough patience. Sometimes I forget he's just a little kid . . . But I love him . . . More than anything in this world I love him.

Monologue Two

JOANNA
(a deep breath, then:)

Ted, when we got married it was because I was twenty-seven years old and I thought I should get married . . . when I had Billy it was because I thought I *should* have a baby . . . and I guess all I did was mess up my life and your life and—

[TED
Joanna, what the hell is—]

JOANNA
(urgent)

Please . . . *Please don't stop me. This* is the hardest thing I've ever had to do . . .

(ON TED—struck by the urgency in her voice.)

After I left . . . When I was in California, I began to think, what kind of mother was I that I could walk out on my own child. It got to where I couldn't tell anybody about Billy—I couldn't stand that look in their faces when I said he wasn't living with me. Finally it seemed like the most important thing in the world to come back here and prove to Billy and to me and to the world how much I loved him . . . And I did . . . And I won. Only . . . it was just another "should."

(She begins to break down.)

Sitting in that courtroom. Hearing everything you did, everything you went through . . . Something happened.

I guess it doesn't matter how much I love him, or how
much you love him. I guess it's like you said, the only thing
that counts is what's best for Billy. I don't know, maybe
that's all love is anyway . . . Ted, I think Billy should stay
with you . . .

> [TED
> *(stunned)*

What?]

> JOANNA
> *(She reaches out, takes his hand.)*

He's already got one mother, he doesn't need two . . .
He's yours . . .

> *(Her last ounce of reserve crumbles.)*

I won't fight you for him any more. He's yours . . .

> [TED

Oh, God . . . Oh, my God . . .]

> JOANNA

Only can I still see him?

Norma Rae

Twentieth Century-Fox/Martin Ritt/Rose and Asseyev, 1979
Screenplay by Irving Ravetch and Harriet Frank, Jr.
Directed by Martin Ritt

Time: 1978
Place: Henleyville, Georgia
Norma Rae Webster, thirty-two, mother of two, has lived
in Henleyville all her life. Like most of the people in town,
she works at O. P. Henley, the local textile mill. The TWUA
(the Textile Workers Union of America) has sent a representative from New York, Reuben Warshovsky, to try to
unionize the mill. Reuben, a city boy, is very much out of

his element in the sleepy Southern town. The townspeople are suspicious and unfriendly: They view Reuben as a troublemaker from the big city.

Monologue One. At a local church Reuben makes his first speech to the citizens of Henleyville, urging them to support a union. Norma Rae is one of the few people attending.

Monologue Two. Norma Rae has gone to work for Reuben and has become his most ardent supporter. In the past weeks she has also managed to get married to a straightforward, kind man, Sonny, who has brought his daughter, Alice, with him. Norma Rae is now the mother of three.

One day at the mill, management posts a notice stating that if the mill is unionized, the black workers will rise up and take over. At Reuben's request Norma Rae copies down the notice as evidence of management's illegal activities. She is ordered to leave the premises, refuses, and, as a result, is arrested. After Reuben posts Norma Rae's bail, she arrives home and goes directly to her kids' room to speak to them.

Monologue One

REUBEN

On October 4, 1970, my grandfather, Isaac Abraham Warshovsky, aged 87, died in his sleep in New York City. On the following Friday morning, his funeral was held. My mother and father attended, my two uncles from Brooklyn attended, my Aunt Minnie came up from Florida. Also present were 862 members of the Amalgamated Clothing Workers and the Cloth, Hat and Cap Makers' Union. Also members of his family. In death as in life, they stood by his side. They had fought battles with him, bound the wounds of battle with him, had earned bread together and had broken it together. When they spoke, they spoke in one

voice, and they were heard. They were black, they were
white, they were Irish, they were Polish, they were Catholic, they were Jews, they were one. That's what a union
is: one.

(pause)

Ladies and gentlemen, the textile industry, in which you
are spending your lives and your substance, and in which
your children and their children will spend their lives and
substance, is the only industry in the whole length and
breadth of the United States of America that is not unionized. Therefore, they are free to exploit you, to cheat
you, to lie to you, and to take away what is rightfully
yours—your health, a decent wage, a fit place to work.
I would urge you to stop them by coming down to room
207 at the Golden Cherry Motel, to pick up a union card
and sign it.

(pauses again)

It comes from the Bible—according to the tribes of your
fathers, ye shall inherit. It comes from Reuben Warshovsky—not unless you make it happen.

Monologue Two

NORMA

Craig, honey, wake up . . . Millie, honey, it's Momma,
get up . . . Alice, sweetheart, come in the other room.

(The CHILDREN get up slowly, rubbing their
eyes. She helps them out of bed, shepherds
them with her back into the other room.
NORMA sits with her children on either side of
her, leaning against her, still half-asleep,
ALICE sprawled in her lap. The two MEN sit
across the room and watch, not intruding.)

I love you children, that's first. And Sonny loves you. You
got both of us. The second thing is, I'm a jailbird. You're

gonna hear that and a lot of other things, but you're gonna hear 'em from me first.

(The CHILDREN look up at her, awake now, alert.)

Millie, your real daddy was named Buddy Wilson and he died four months after you were born. Craig, I never was married to your daddy, and your daddy was not Sonny and not Buddy, but another man. And there were some others in my life and they'll be telling you about them, too.

(reaches into the box, takes out papers and photographs)

I got pictures of Craig's father in here for him, and pictures of Millie's father for her. Craig, I got settlement papers in here made between me and your daddy; this is your stuff. It's not mine, it's yours. It's your life.

(puts the papers in his lap)

I want you to feel there's nothing you can't come to me and talk to me about. If you go into the mill, I want life to be better for you than it is for me; that's why I joined up with the union and got fired for it. I'm not making excuses for myself—like everybody else, I'm not perfect and I made these mistakes. But I hope you'll learn from my experiences that life has a meaning; there is a moral reason for why you should do this and why you shouldn't do this.

(pauses)

Now you kids know that I've cleaned out my closet. You know what I am and you know that I believe in standing up for my rights.

(She hugs them each in turn, and they hug her back.)

Go to the bathroom before you go back to bed.

Apocalypse Now

Omni Zoetrope (Produced by Francis Ford Coppola), 1979
Screenplay by John Milius,
Francis Ford Coppola, and Michael Herr
Directed by Francis Ford Coppola

Time: 1970s
Place: Cambodia
The Vietnam war is in progress. Frank Willard is with the
Army Special Forces. His assignment is to go up the Nung
River, find and "terminate" Captain Walter Kurtz. Kurtz
was one of the most outstanding officers in the Army. He is
now wanted for murder, because he ordered the unauthor-
ized execution of some Vietnamese soldiers that he took for
double agents. Deserting the Army, he has collected a band
of devoted followers, most of them Vietnamese, who obey
his every command and think of him as a kind of god. He
rules his mini-kingdom in the jungle with a tyrannical hand.

When Willard finally reaches Kurtz, Kurtz's men capture
and torture him. Throughout the ordeal Willard remains
strong. Kurtz is impressed by Willard's resolve and frees
him from his bamboo prison. Kurtz knows that Willard
has been sent to assassinate him but makes no move to kill
him, allowing him to move unrestricted throughout Kurtz's
castlelike domain.

One rainy night, while Willard crouches nearby, Kurtz
speaks.

―――――

KURTZ

I've seen the horror. Horrors that you've seen. But you
have no right to call me a murderer. You have a right to
kill me. You have a right to do that, but you have no right
to judge me. It's impossible for words to describe what is

necessary to those who do not know what horror means. Horror. Horror has a face, and you must make a friend of horror. Horror and moral terror are your friends. If they are not, then they are enemies to be feared. They are truly enemies.

(pause)

I remember when I was with Special Forces—it seems a thousand centuries ago—we went into a camp to inoculate it. The children. We left the camp after we had inoculated the children for polio, and this old man came running after us, and he was crying. He couldn't see. We went back there, and they had come and hacked off every inoculated arm. There they were in a pile—a pile of little arms. And I remember . . . I . . . I . . . I cried, I wept like some grandmother. I wanted to tear my teeth out, I didn't know what I wanted to do. And I want to remember it, I never want to forget it. I never want to forget. And then I realized—like I was *shot* . . . like I was *shot* with a diamond . . . a diamond bullet right through my forehead. And I thought, "My God, the genius of that, the genius, the will to do that." Perfect, genuine, complete, crystalline, pure. And then I realized they were stronger than we, because they could stand that—these were not monsters, these were men, trained contras, these men who fought with their hearts, who have families, who have children, who are filled with love—that they had this strength, the *strength* to do that. If I had ten divisions of those men, then our troubles here would be over very quickly. You have to have men who are moral and at the same time were able to utilize their primordial instincts to kill without feeling, without passion, without judgment—without *judgment*. Because it's judgment that defeats us.

(pause)

I worry that my son might not understand what I've tried to be, and if I were to be killed, Willard, I would want someone to go to my home and tell my son everything. Everything I did, everything you saw, because there's nothing that I detest more than the stench of lies. And if you understand me, Willard, you . . . you will do this for me.

Breaking Away

Twentieth Century-Fox (Produced by Peter Yates), 1979
Screenplay by Steve Tesich
Directed by Peter Yates

Time: 1979
Place: Bloomington, Indiana—on the edge of the University of Indiana campus
In the university town of Bloomington, the kids who were born and raised in the town are called "cutters," because, for generations, the workingmen of the area have made their living cutting limestone out of the rich quarries of Indiana. The college kids use the term "cutter," however, in a disparaging way. They feel superior to the local kids who, after high school, usually go on to blue-collar jobs.

Dave, Mike, Cyril, and Moocher are seniors in the local high school and fed up with the college kids' attitude. One night, at dusk, the four friends are sitting in Mike's car. Mike speaks.

MIKE

I really thought I was a great quarterback in high school. I still think so. I can't even bring myself to light a cigarette 'cause I keep thinking I should stay in shape. And you know what gets me? Living here and reading in the papers how some hotshot college kid is the new star on the college

team. Every year there'll be a new one and it's never going
to be me. I'll just be Mike. Twenty-year-old Mike. Thirty-
year-old Mike. Old mean old man Mike. But the college
kids will never get old . . . out of shape . . . 'cause new
ones come every year. And they'll keep calling us 'cutters!'
To them, it's a dirty word, but to me it'll just be something
else I never got a chance to be.

*(He falls silent and sticks a cigarette in his
mouth.)*

The Great Santini

Warners/Orion/Bing Crosby Productions, 1979
Screenplay by Lewis John Carlino
Based on the novel by Pat Conroy
Directed by Lewis John Carlino

Time: 1962
Place: Primarily Beaufort, South Carolina
Colonel "Bull" Meechum is in his forties and the training
commander of a crack squad of Marine Corps pilots. He
has a family—wife Lillian and four children. The oldest
child, Ben, is turning eighteen and able to judge and challenge his father.

"Bull" commands through skill and experience but also
through sheer force of personality. He is strongly committed to the Marine Air Corps—his flyers—and to his family.

In fact, he relates to his wife and children in much the
same way he deals with his young training pilots. He loves
but must dominate—holding his family to the highest stan-
dards. His men and his family love him with equal touches
of fear, awe, and exasperation, but their love is genuine.

Monologue One. "Bull" welcomes a new trainee.

Monologue Two. "Bull" prepares his family for a move to a new town, new house, new school, and new friends and neighbors.

Monologue One

BULL

Good morning. You men now have the privilege of serving under the meanest, toughest, screamingest squadron commander in the Marine Corps. *Me!* In the next couple of months you're gonna do things with jet planes you never thought possible. You are going to get so good at flying the F-4, you're gonna forget your wives and kids, your homes, and the fact that the Red Sox are going to win the American League pennant. Now I don't want you to consider me as just your commanding officer. I want you to look on me like I was . . . well . . . *God*. If I say something, you pretend it's coming from the burning bush. We are members of the proudest, most elite group of fighting men in the world. We are Marines! Marine Corps fighter pilots! We have no other function. That is our mission and you are either going to hack it or pack it. Do you read me?

(The men sit transfixed. There is no coughing or shuffling.)

Within thirty days I am going to lead the toughest, flyingest sons-of-bitches in the world. The 367th Werewolf Squadron is going to make history, or it will die trying. You're flying with Bull Meechum now and I kid you not, this is the eye of the storm. Welcome aboard.

Monologue Two

BULL

Okay, hogs, I've listened to you bellyache about moving to this new town. This said bellyaching will end as of 0859

hours, and will not affect the morale of the squadron hence-
forth. Do I make myself clear?

(The CHILDREN nod.)

Now I know it's rough to leave your friends and move every
year, but you are Marine kids and can chew nails while
other kids are sucking cotton candy. And you are Mee-
chums. A Meechum is a thoroughbred, a winner all the
way. He gets the best grades, wins the most awards, and
excels in sports. A Meechum never gives up. I want you
hogs to let this burg know you're here. I want these crackers
to wake up and wonder what the hell blew into town. And
one more thing. Just because a Meechum has more raw
talent than anyone else, that doesn't prevent him from
thinking about the Man Upstairs every once in a while.
Don't be too proud to ask for His help.

(The SOUND of a HORN HONKING turns
him around. A moving van approaches the
house. BULL looks at his watch.)

Right on time. Okay, hogs, by nightfall I want this camp
in inspection order. Do you *read me loud and clear?*

[THE CHILDREN

Yes, *sir!*]

BULL

(to Ben)

Sergeant, dismiss the troops.

———————————————————————

Manhattan

United Artists/A Jack Rollins—
Charles H. Joffe Production, 1979
Screenplay by Woody Allen and Marshall Brickman
Directed by Woody Allen

Time: 1979–1980
Place: Manhattan
Isaac (Ike) Davis, forty-two, is a successful television comedy writer attempting a novel. Divorced twice, Ike is the father of a young boy who lives with ex-wife Jill and her lesbian lover. Jill is writing a book in large part about the breakup of her marriage to Ike, causing him no end of anxiety.

Ike is having an unlikely but heartfelt love affair with Tracy, a beautiful seventeen-year-old high-school senior. His life is further complicated when he becomes involved with Mary Wilke, also divorced, a high-strung, very bright, free-lance journalist in her thirties. Mary is having an on-again off-again affair with Ike's best friend, Yale, a married academic.

At one point, Ike dictates into his tape recorder: "An idea for a short story . . . *(sighing)* about . . . people in Manhattan who . . . are constantly creating these real . . . unnecessary neurotic problems for themselves 'cause it keeps them from dealing with . . . more unsolvable, terrifying problems about . . . the universe."

At the beginning of the film, however, Ike tries a few upbeat openings for his novel.

———

IKE

"Chapter One. He adored New York City. He idolized it all out of proportion." Uh, no, make that: "He—he

. . . romanticized it all out of proportion. Now . . . to him . . . no matter what the season was, this was still a town that existed in black and white and pulsated to the great tunes of George Gershwin." Ahhh, now let me start this over. "Chapter One. He was too romantic about Manhattan as he was about everything else. He thrived on the hustle . . . bustle of the crowds and the traffic. To him, New York meant beautiful women and street-smart guys who seemed to know all the angles." Nah, no . . . corny, too corny . . . for . . . my taste.

(clearing his throat)

I mean, let me try and make it more profound. "Chapter One. He adored New York City. To him, it was a metaphor for the decay of contemporary culture. The same lack of individual integrity to cause so many people to take the easy way out . . . was rapidly turning the town of his dreams in—" No, it's gonna be too preachy. I mean, you know . . . let's face it, I wanna sell some books here. "Chapter One. He adored New York City, although to him, it was a metaphor for the decay of contemporary culture. How hard it was to exist in a society desensitized by drugs, loud music, television, crime, garbage." Too angry. I don't wanna be angry. "Chapter One. He was as . . . tough and romantic as the city he loved. Behind his black-rimmed glasses was the coiled sexual power of a jungle cat." I love this. "New York was his town. And it always would be."

Stardust Memories

United Artists/A Jack Rollins–
Charles H. Joffe Production, 1980
Screenplay by Woody Allen
Directed by Woody Allen

Time: 1980

Place: Stardust Hotel in New Jersey

Sandy Bates, a film director and writer in his early forties, is adored and revered by his fans and tired of it all. Someone is heard complaining: "What does he have to suffer about? Doesn't the man know he's got the greatest gift that anyone could have? The gift of laughter."

But Sandy Bates is suffering and holding court as best he can at a weekend festival of his films at the Stardust Hotel in New Jersey. The hotel scene is a "carnival-of-animals" affair with fans, old friends, and old lovers.

Over the weekend three beautiful women weave their way through Sandy's life and memory. Dorrie, a former lover, dark-haired, worldly, sensual, is prone to nervous breakdowns. Isobel, a blond Frenchwoman, maternal, earthy and serene, the mother of young children, cannot commit to Sandy. And there is Daisy, a neurotic, brilliant concert violinist in her twenties who is brought to the weekend festival by a screenwriting instructor.

The instructor introduces Daisy to Sandy, and Sandy finds himself attracted to her. She reminds him of Dorrie somehow. He tells Daisy, later, that both she and Dorrie are "seductive and attractive . . . beautiful, and . . . [have] not a tragic sense . . . but . . . a lost feeling."

At one point during the weekend Sandy is sitting in a phone booth at the hotel, talking with a business associate. After he hangs up he overhears Daisy, in the next booth, talking to someone.

DAISY
(offscreen, into the telephone)

God, the thing is, though—God, I'm crazy right now. I just . . . just—I don't seem to be able to sleep, you know? I—I—I have to do—do some practicing on the violin, 'cause I gotta go back to the Philharmonic in a couple of weeks. But, uh, you know, I—I— Last night I had a migraine, and I—so I took some, some Darvon and—and—and that made me so nervous that I—took, I took, uh, forty milligrams of Valium . . .

(The camera moves from SANDY to DAISY, no longer wearing her sunglasses, in her phone booth. She is talking into the receiver, almost cradling it as she smokes a cigarette. She touches her mouth.)

—you know, and then I—and I still couldn't sleep. I was up all night . . . Yeah . . . Well, well, I got a message on my service that Sarah called . . . Yeah, I know, I haven't talked to her in about a year, you know, and uh, I—I—I—I got upset. I started eating. I ate a pound of cookies last night— Yeah, I'm really fat. Really fat. And, uh, J-Jack, um, Jack was so sweet about it . . . No, he—he, no, he doesn't know about my relationship with her. I mean, he knows that we lived together in Israel, but he doesn't—he doesn't know that—He—he was so affectionate last night, in—in bed, you know, he wanted—I—I told him I had herpes . . .

(pausing)

Yeah . . . Well, no, uh, take the—the call, I'll hold on— I'll hold on a second.

Raging Bull

United Artists/Chartoff-Winkler, 1980
Screenplay by Paul Schrader and Mardik Martin
Directed by Martin Scorsese

Time: 1940s through 1960s
Place: New York
Raging Bull is the story of the rise and decline of Jake La
Motta, who was the world middleweight boxing champion
during the late 1940s. La Motta was eventually suspended
from boxing when the authorities accused him of throwing
a fight. He ends up, in the 1960s, doing a comedy nightclub
act and reciting dramatic literature.

Joey, Jake's older brother, was Jake's manager. This
monologue occurs one day in the 1940s around Jake's
kitchen table. Joey wants to help him gain a shot at the
title.

――――――

JOEY
(*yelling*)

This Janiro's an up-and-coming fighter, this kid you gotta
knock out. Knock out this fuckin' kid! I'm telling you, this
is your step towards getting a shot at the title. Listen to
me: I'm telling you. You been killin' yourself for three years.
There's nobody left—they're afraid to fight you. This Janiro's up-and-coming. He don't know. Fuckin' tear him apart,
wipe him out! What are you worried about? Your weight?
Look, even if you *lose* they're gonna think you're weak;
they're gonna think you're not the fighter you used to be.
They'll match you with guys they were afraid to match you
with before, and then you'll kill them and you'll get your
title shot. And if you beat this kid Janiro, they *gotta* give
you a shot at the title because there's nobody else. Either

way you win and you do it on your own—just like you want
it. All right?

The French Lieutenant's Woman

United Artists/Juniper (Produced by Leon Clore), 1981
Screenplay by Harold Pinter
Based on the novel by John Fowles
Directed by Karel Reisz

Time: 1867
Place: Lyme, England
Sarah Woodruff, around thirty, used to work in Charmouth
as a governess for the Talbot family. While working there
Sarah met a French lieutenant who was brought wounded
to the house. Over the course of several weeks Sarah nursed
him back to health. When he recovered, he left for Weymouth, and Sarah followed him there. In Weymouth she
discovered that he was insincere and did not truly love her.
She returned to Charmouth severely depressed and unable
to continue her job as governess. Now Sarah works as a
secretary and companion for Mrs. Poulteney, an elderly
widow.

One day, while on the edge of the sea rampart in Lyme,
Sarah encounters Charles Smithson, a thiry-two-year-old
paleontologist from the upper class who is walking down
the quay with his fiancée. Although Charles only speaks to
Sarah, warning her of a storm and sudden wind, it is clear
that he is deeply affected by her presence.

The two meet again a number of times in the Undercliff,
a wooded area near Lyme. During one such encounter
Charles tells Sarah that for them to continue to meet alone
would be improper. Sarah begs him for just one final hour

of his time, so that she can tell him the story of what happened to her eighteen months ago in Weymouth.

SARAH

His name was Varguennes. He was brought to the house after the wreck of his ship. He had a dreadful wound. His flesh was torn from his hip to his knee. He was in great pain. Yet he never cried out. Not the smallest groan. I admired his courage. I looked after him. I did not know then that men can be both very brave and very false.

(pause)

He was handsome. No man had ever paid me the kind of attentions he did, as he . . . was recovering. He told me I was beautiful, that he could not understand why I was not married. Such things. He would . . . mock me, lightly.

(pause)

I took pleasure in it.

(pause)

When I would not let him kiss my hand he called me cruel. A day came when I thought myself cruel as well.

(fiercely)

You cannot understand, Mr. Smithson. Because you are not a woman. You are not a woman born to be a farmer's wife but educated to be something . . . better. You were not born a woman with a love of intelligence, beauty, learning, but whose position in the world forbids her to share this love with another. And you are not the daughter of a bankrupt. You have not spent your life in penury. You are not . . . condemned. You are not an outcast. Varguennes recovered. He asked me to go back with him to France. He offered me . . . marriage. He left for Weymouth. He said he would wait there one week and then sail for France. I said I would never follow him, that I could not.

But . . . after he had gone . . . my loneliness was so deep,
I felt I would drown in it.

(pause)

I followed him. I went to the Inn where he had taken a
room. It was not . . . a respectable place. I knew that at
once. They told me to go up to his room. They looked at
me . . . and smiled. I insisted he be sent for. He seemed
overjoyed to see me. He was all that a lover should be. I
had not eaten that day. He took me . . . to a private sitting
room, ordered food.

(pause)

But he had changed. He was full of smiles and caresses but
I knew at once that he was insincere. I saw that I had been
an amusement for him, nothing more. He was a liar. I saw
all this within five minutes of our meeting.

(pause)

Yet I stayed. I ate the supper that was served. I drank the
wine he pressed on me. It did not intoxicate me. I think
it made me see more clearly. Is that possible?

(pause)

Soon he no longer bothered to hide the real nature of his
intentions towards me. Nor could I pretend surprise. My
innocence was false from the moment I chose to stay. I
could tell you that he overpowered me, that he drugged
me. But it is not so.

(She looks at him directly.)

I gave myself to him.

(silence)

I did it . . . so that I should never be the same again, so
that I should be seen for the outcast I am. I knew it was
ordained that I could never marry an equal. So I married
shame. It is my shame . . . that has kept me alive, my
knowing that I am truly not like other women. I shall never
like them have children, a husband, the pleasures of a
home. Sometimes I pity them. I have a freedom they cannot

understand. No insult, no blame, can touch me. I have set myself beyond the pale. I am nothing. I am hardly human any more. I am the French Lieutenant's Whore.

My Dinner with Andre

Andre Company/George W. George/Michael White, 1981
Screenplay by Wallace Shawn and Andre Gregory
Directed by Louis Malle

Time: 1981
Place: Manhattan restaurant
Two friends who have not seen each other in a long time meet for dinner. One, Andre, is an avant-garde theater director. The other, Wally, is a struggling actor and playwright.

Andre is looking for "a new language, a language of the heart . . . where language [isn't] needed . . . and in order to create that language, we're going to have to learn how [to] go through a looking-glass into another kind of perception . . . and suddenly you understand everything"— something sacred and redeeming.

Andre travels the world in search of this new language. He visits experimental outposts: a Polish forest inhabited by Grotowski's disciples; a community in northern Scotland dedicated to meditation, education, and interplanetary communication; and the Sahara desert.

Though Andre does most of the talking, Wally responds at one point to Andre's stories of utopian and mystical attempts to change the world.

Note: When Wally mentions stones, he's referring to an experience Andre had in Scotland. Andre says he worked with members of a group to keep strong gales there from blowing the roof off their headquarters by placing large beach stones on a roof *not* joined to the building in the usual way. Even though experts say the roof should blow off, it doesn't. Andre is amazed and sees this as a sign of the magical.

When Wally mentions the flag, he's referring to another of Andre's stories. Andre told him about having a flag made for a group in India he was going to visit. The flag maker created a flag with the ancient symbol from Tibet, the Tibetan swastika, which is not the Nazi swastika but which still had a horrible effect on whomever came into contact with it—it was later burned in a ceremony.

When Wally mentions handprints, he's referring to Andre's epiphany at discovering surreal connections in an issue of the surrealist magazine from the twenties and thirties, *Minotaur*. At random, Andre picked an issue and, also at random, opened to a full-page reproduction of the letter *A* from Tenniel's illustration of the story of "Alice in Wonderland," which was the great theater work that Andre directed in the 1960s in New York City. The next page he turns to has four handprints—all of famous, creative French men whose names begin with *A*, one of whom, Antoine de Saint-Exupéry, wrote *The Little Prince*, which Andre was beginning to work on as a theater piece. Other such "coincidences" and revelations follow: Andre was born the day the issue of the magazine was being delivered to the newsstands.

Wally tries to explain his reaction to this kind of thinking. At one earlier point he says, "But, Andre . . . isn't it a little upsetting to come to the conclusion that there's no way to wake people up anymore except to involve them in some strange kind of christening in Poland or some kind of strange experience on top of Mount Everest? Because, I mean, the awful thing is—let's face it, Andre— . . . everybody can't be taken to Everest."

WALLY

Yeah. Well, you see— Well, Andre, you know, if you want to know my *actual* response to all this—do you want to hear my actual response?

[ANDRE

Yes!]

WALLY

Well, Andre, I mean, my *actual* response—I mean, Andre, really—I'm just trying to survive—you know? I mean, I'm trying to earn a living, I'm trying to pay my rent and my bills. I mean, I live my life, I enjoy staying home with Debby, I'm reading Charlton Heston's autobiogrphy, and that's that.

(pause)

I mean, occasionally, maybe, Debby and I will step outside and we'll go to a party or something, and if I can occasionally get my little talent together and write a play, well then that's wonderful, and I enjoy reading about other little plays that people have written, and reading the reviews of those plays and what people said about them, and what people said about what people said. And I mean, I have a list of errands and responsibilities that I keep in a notebook, and I enjoy going through my list and carrying out the responsibilities and doing the errands and then crossing them off my list. And I mean, I just don't know how anybody could enjoy anything *more* than I enjoy reading Charlton Heston's autobiography and, you know, getting up in the morning and having the cup of cold coffee that's been waiting for me all night *still there* for me to drink in the morning, and no cockroach or fly has died in it overnight—I'm just so *thrilled* when I get up, and I see that coffee there, just the way I want it, I just can't imagine enjoying something else any more than that. I mean, obviously if the cockroach— if there *is* a dead cockroach in it, then I just have a feeling of disappointment, and I'm sad. But I mean, I don't think I feel the need for anything more than all this. Whereas you seem to be saying that it's inconceivable that anybody could be having a meaningful life today, and everyone is totally destroyed, and we need to live in these outposts— But I mean, even for you, I just can't believe—I mean, don't you find—isn't it pleasant just to get up in the morning, and there's Chiquita, there are the children, the *Times* is delivered, you can read it, and—maybe you'll direct a play, maybe you *won't* direct a play, but forget about the play that you may or may not direct—why is it necessary to—why not lean back and just *enjoy* these details? I mean, and there would be a delicious cup of coffee, and a piece of coffee cake. I mean, why is it necessary to have *more* than this, or to even *think* about having more than this? I mean, I don't *really* know what you're talking about. I mean, I know what you're talking about, but I don't *really* know what you're talking about. And I mean, actually, even if I *did* feel the way you do—you know, that there's no possibility for happiness now—then, frankly, I *still* couldn't accept the idea that the way to make life wonderful would be to totally reject Western civilization and to fall back into a kind of belief in some kind of weird something. I mean— I mean, I don't even know how to begin talking about this, but I mean—I mean, you know, in the Middle Ages, before the arrival of scientific thinking as we know it today, well, people could believe *anything*—*anything* could be true— a statue of the Virgin Mary *could* speak or bleed or whatever. But the wonderful thing that happened was that then in the development of science in the Western world certain things *did* come slowly to be known and understood. I mean, of *course* all ideas in science are constantly being revised—I mean, that's the whole point—but we do at least know that the universe has *some* shape and order and that, you know, trees do *not* turn into people or goddesses, and there are very good reasons *why* they don't, and you can't just believe absolutely anything. And I mean, the things you're talking about—I mean, either the stones have the weight to hold down that roof, or they don't. And I mean, when you talk about things like that flag or the handprints— I mean, you seem constantly to be finding a significance in these things that to me are just *facts*. I mean, you found the handprints in the book, and they were three Andres and one Antoine de Saint-Exupéry. And to me that is a coincidence. And the people who put that book together had their own reasons for putting it together. But to you it was significant, as if that book had been written forty years ago so that you would see it—as if it was planned for you in a way. I mean, really—I mean, Andre, let's say— I mean, if I get a fortune cookie in a Chinese restaurant, I mean, of *course* even *I* have a tendency—I mean, *you* know, I would hardly throw it out—I mean, I read it, I read it, and I—I just instinctively sort of—if it says something like—uh—a conversation with a dark-haired man will be very important for you, I mean, I just instinctively think, Well, who do I know who has dark hair, and did we have a conversation, and what did we talk about? In other words, I mean, I do tend to read it—but it's a joke, in my mind. I mean, in other words, there's something in me that makes me read it, and I instinctively interpret it as if it really were an omen of the future. But in my *conscious* opinion, which is so fundamental to my whole view of life—I mean, I would have to change totally, I think, to not have this opinion— in my *conscious* opinion, this is simply something that was written in the cookie factory several years ago and in no way refers to me. I mean, the fact that I got it—the man who wrote it did not know anything about me, couldn't have known anything about me. There's no way that this cookie could actually have anything to do with me. The fact that I've gotten it is basically a joke. And I mean, if I were planning to go on a trip on an airplane, and I got a fortune cookie that said "Don't go," I mean I admit I might feel a bit nervous for about one second, but in fact I would go, because I mean, that trip is going to be successful or unsuccessful based on the state of the airplane and the state of the pilot. And the cookie is in no position to know about that. And it's the same with any kind of prophecy or sign or omen. Because if you believe in omens, then that means that the universe—I can hardly begin to describe this— that somehow the future can send messages backward to the present. Which means that the future exists in some sense already in order to be able to send these messages. And it also means that things in the universe are there for a purpose, to give us messages. Whereas I believe that things in the universe are just there. They don't mean anything. I mean, if the turtle's egg falls out of the tree and splashes on the paving stones, it's just because that turtle was clumsy by accident. And to decide whether to send my ships to war on the basis of that seems a big mistake to me.

An Officer and a Gentleman

Paramount/Lorimar (Produced by Martin Elfand), 1982
Screenplay by Douglas Day Stewart
Directed by Taylor Hackford

Time: 1982
Place: Puget Sound, Washington State
Puget Sound is the site of one of the country's pilot training schools where many young men and women start their journey to become naval aviators. Gunnery Sergeant Foley is in charge of the new recruits. In this monologue he

addresses his new class of cadets on their first day at the Academy.

FOLEY
(screams)
Fall in! Form a line, you slimy worms! Toes on that chalk line! I said toes on the chalk line! Attin-hut!
(still screaming)
I don't believe what I'm seeing! Where've you been all your lives, at an orgy? Listening to Mick Jagger and bad mouthing your country, I'll bet.
(His voice shifts register, becoming almost human.)
(a sudden grin)
I know why most of you are here. We're not stupid. But before you get to sell what we teach you over at United Airlines, you gotta give the Navy six years of your life, Sweet Pea. Lots of things can happen in six years. Another war could come up in six years. If you're too peaceful a person to dump napalm on an enemy village where there might be women and children, I'm gonna find that out . . . understand?
(beat)
I expect to lose half of you before I'm finished. I will use every means at my disposal, fair or unfair, to trip you up, expose your weaknesses . . . as a potential aviator . . . and as a human being. Understand? The prize at the other end is a flight education worth one million dollars, but first you have to get past me.

Fanny and Alexander

AB Cinematograph/Swedish Film Institute/Swedish TV One/
Gaumont/Persona Film/Tobis (Produced by Jorn Donner),
1982
Screenplay by Ingmar Bergman
Directed by Ingmar Bergman

Time: 1907
Place: Uppsala, Sweden
A large, distinguished, and prosperous theatrical family,
the Ekdahls, preside over the extended familial world of
the theater in their city, a medieval university town on a
river. The Ekdahls have run and performed in the theater
there for generations.

Mrs. Helena Ekdahl, a widow and former actress, is the
matriarch of the family. Her eldest son, Oscar, the theater's
impresario, is married to a beautiful actress, Emilie Ekdahl,
the mother of three children who may not be Oscar's—
Amanda, 12, Alexander, 10, and Fanny, 8. Carl Ekdahl
is Helena's second son, a professor married to Lydia,
German-born and still, to Carl's dismay, speaking German before Swedish. Carl is unfaithful to Lydia but depends on her nevertheless.

Monologue One. Carl, a mediocre academic living in the
Ekdahl house, complains to his wife.

Monologue Two. Fanny and Alexander's mother, Emilie,
in her late twenties, is suddenly confronted by the death
of her husband, Oscar, a much loved but much older man.
He dies leaving her with the children. She eventually marries Bishop Edvard Vergerus, a stern, dangerously fanatic
pastor, who dominates her and the children with austere,
overly strict discipline. She slips away briefly one day from
his family's medieval stone-cold castle to see her mother-

in-law, Helena, at the Ekdahl house in the country and confesses that life with Edvard has been a mistake.

Monologue Three. Helena's good friend and former lover, Isak, a Jewish antique dealer, and his family help Emilie, Fanny, and Alexander escape from the pastor. Fanny and Alexander find themselves in an exotic world at Isak's house, filled with unusual treasures and even an Egyptian mummy in a case. Aron, about twenty years old, Isak's nephew, takes Alexander on a late-night tour of the mysteries and curiosities of this place. Ismael, Aron's younger brother, is locked up and hidden away in one of the rooms. Alexander is frightened, then intrigued and enchanted, as Aron speaks.

Monologue One

CARL

The head of the faculty takes me to task and says I neglect my lectures. But I'm a scientist. I'm the only real scientist in this whole damned university. But nobody cares. The publishers didn't print my last paper. It was ill-founded, if you please. They only say that because I don't lick the other professors' boots. I feel ill. There was something wrong with the herring salad; it tasted stale. You can be sure the stingy old crone has been saving it since Easter. No one bloody well eats herring salad at Christmas. God, my head. I've a frightful headache. What am I to do? I must sleep. We have to go to that confounded early service too. Nothing but compulsion. Compulsion everywhere. And one must smile and be polite: "Dear Mama, how pretty you are today. You look like a young girl. Emilie dear, you've never played your Christmas angel so beautifully. How is it you succeed in everything you undertake, Brother Oscar?" How do you do it?

(wearily)

How do you do it? How is it one becomes second-rate, can you answer me that? How does the dust fall? When has one lost? First I'm a prince, the heir to the kingdom. Suddenly, before I know it, I am deposed. Death taps me on the shoulder. The room is cold and we can't pay for the wood. I'm ugly and unkind. And I'm unkindest to the one person who cares for me. You can never forgive me. I'm a shit and a rotter.

Monologue Two

EMILIE

I have been away too long.

(shaking her head)

It's worst for the children. They are punished for the slightest misdemeanor. Henrietta locks them in and forces them to go to bed in the middle of the day. A week ago Fanny refused to eat up her porridge. She was made to sit there all evening. She was sick at the table. At last she ate it. Alexander is mad with jealousy but doesn't realize it is mutual. I am tormented by a boundless self-contempt. How could I be so blind? How could I feel sorry for that man? After all I'm an actress and should have seen through his dissimulation. But he was cleverer than I was. His conviction was greater than mine and he dazzled me. I had been living alone so long, ever since Fanny's birth. I hated my occasional emotional storms. I hated the terrible loneliness of my body. Oscar was my best friend, you know that, Helena. You know how fond of him I was; you know that my grief was sincere when he left us. But you also know that we never touched each other . . . I thought that my life was finished, sealed up. Sometimes I grieved, but blamed myself for my ingratitude. What is the time, Helena? I must go soon; I'm so afraid of being late. His rage is terrible.

I don't know how a man can live with so much hate. I saw nothing; I was too dense. He spoke to me of another life—a life of demands, of purity, of joy in the performance of duty. I had never heard such words. There seemed to be a light around him when he talked to me. At the same time I saw that he was lonely, that he was unhappy, haunted by fear and bad dreams. He assured me that I would save him. He said that together with the children we would live a life in God's nearness—in the truth. *That* was the most important, I think—what he said about the truth. I was so thirsty—it sounds dramatic and overstrung, Helena, I know, but I can't find any other word—I thirsted for the truth. I felt I had been living a lie. I also knew that the children needed a father who could support them and guide them with a firm hand.

(pause)

He would also free me from my physical loneliness. I was so grateful, Helena. And I left my old life without regret. Now I must go. A carriage is waiting up by the gate. I am afraid that something may have happened while I have been here. I go in constant dread that Alexander may say something that displeases him. Alexander is so foolhardy. I have tried to warn him, but he can't see that his stepfather is a dangerous opponent who is merely waiting for the right opportunity to crush him. Every hour I think I ought to leave him, sue for a divorce, go back to the theater and our family.

Monologue Three

ARON

Don't cry, Alexander, I didn't mean to frighten you. At least not much. I've been sitting all night working on that puppet—there's a wealthy circus owner in England who is mad about our puppets. Then I heard you tiptoeing about.

(listens)

Quiet. Do you hear? Now my brother Ismael is awake. Can you hear? He's singing. Poor Ismael! Human beings are more than he can bear. Sometimes he gets violent and then he's dangerous. Come along, we'll go and see him. The doctors say that his intelligence is far above the normal. He never stops reading. He's incredibly learned and knows everything by heart. Would you like a cup of coffee, Alexander? Or a slice of bread? Shall I heat some milk for you? There is much that is strange and cannot be explained. You notice that particularly when you dabble in magic. Have you seen our mummy? Look carefully, Alexander. Can you see it breathing? It has been dead for more than four thousand years but it breathes. I'll make the room dark. What do you see? No one knows why it is luminous. Dozens of learned men have been here and examined the old lady both outside and inside, but they can't explain why she shines. Anything unintelligible makes people angry. It's much better to blame the apparatus and the mirrors and the projections. Then people start laughing and that's healthier from all points of view—particularly the financial one. My father and mother ran a conjurer's theater in Petersburg. That's why I know what I'm talking about. One evening, in the middle of the performance, a real ghost appeared, an aunt of my father's. She had died two days earlier. The ghost lost her way among the machines and the projectors. It was a fiasco and Papa had to refund the admission. Uncle Isak says we are surrounded by realities, one outside the other. He says that there are swarms of ghosts, spirits, phantoms, souls, poltergeists, demons, angels, and devils. He says that the smallest pebble has a life of its own.

(pouring it out)

Everything is alive. Everything is God or God's thought,

not only what is good but also the cruelest things. What do *you* think?

Poltergeist

MGM/SLM (Produced by Steven Spielberg), 1982
Screenplay by Steven Spielberg,
Michael Grais, and Mark Victor
Directed by Tobe Hooper

Time: 1982
Place: Southern California
The Freelings live in a middle-class housing development called Cuesta Verdes. Steven, the father, works as a salesman for the company that built the development. Diane, the mother, takes care of their children, Dana, 16; Robert, 8; and Carol Anne, 5.

One evening the family discovers Carol Anne talking to something in the TV downstairs, which has been left on after the "sign-off." The next day Carol Anne wakes up in the middle of the night and again stares at the "snow" on the TV, this time announcing to her parents and brother that "they're here."

In the morning it is clear that there is a supernatural force, a poltergeist, loose in the Freeling house. Silverware bends, chairs mysteriously pile up in a pyramid formation, and Carol Anne can slide across the floor unaided.

When Carol Anne disappears, the Freelings hire a parapsychologist, Dr. Lesh, to find her. Dr. Lesh brings Tangina, a clairvoyant, to the Freeling house. Tangina is a woman with a special knowledge of spirits. She has "cleaned" many houses. Tangina tells Diane that Carol Anne is alive and in the house and that she is trapped in another dimension of time and space. The point of origin of this dimension is Carol Anne's closet.

Before Tangina agrees to let Diane in the closet to rescue Carol Anne, Tangina speaks.

TANGINA

Would you all come on in? Gather round. There is no death; there is only a transition to a different sphere of consciousness. Carol Ann is not like those she's with. She's a living presence in their spiritual, earth-bound plane. They are attracted to the one thing about her that's different from themselves . . . her life force—it is very strong, it gives off its own illumination, it is a light that implies life and memory of love and home and earthly pleasures—something they desperately desire but can't have anymore. Right now she's the closest thing to that and that is a terrible distraction from the real light that has finally come for them. Do you understand me? These souls, who, for whatever reason, are not at rest, are also not aware that they've passed on . . . they're not part of consciousness as we know it— they linger in a perpetual dream state, a nightmare from which they cannot wake. Inside this spectral light is salvation, a window to the next plane. They must pass through this membrane where friends are waiting to guide them to new destinies. Carol Ann must help them cross over, and she will only hear her mother's voice. Now, hold on to yourselves, there's one more thing. A terrible presence is in there with her . . . so much rage, so much betrayal. I've never sensed anything like it. I don't know what hovers over this house, but it was strong enough to punch a hole into this world and take your daughter away from you. It keeps Carol Ann very close to it and away from the spectral light. It lies to her, it says things only a child can understand. It has been using her to restrain the others. To her it simply is another child, to us it is the beast. Now, let's go get your daughter.

Diner

MGM/SLM (Produced by Jerry Weintraub), 1982
Screenplay by Barry Levinson
Directed by Barry Levinson

Time: 1959
Place: Baltimore, Maryland

A group of six high-school friends get together around the Christmas/New Year holidays. Most of them have stayed in town after graduation. Shrevie, the first of the group to get married, works in an appliance store and nurtures his obsession for his record collection. He can tell you what's on the flip side of practically every record he owns. His collection is kept in frighteningly fastidious condition—with a detailed system of categories that would put the Library of Congress to shame.

Eddie, his pal, a ferociously loyal Baltimore Colts fan, is planning on marrying Elise on New Year's Eve on the condition that she pass an outrageously difficult football quiz he has prepared for her. One night, in front of the local diner where the guys hang out, two days before the test, three days before the wedding, Eddie asks Shrevie if he's happy with his marriage to *his* wife, Beth. Shrevie answers.

SHREVIE
You know the big part of the problem? When we were dating we spent most of our time talking about sex. *Why*

couldn't I do it? *Where* could we do it? Were her parents
going to be out *so* we could do it. Talking about being alone
for a weekend. A whole night. You know. Everything was
talking about gettin' sex or planning our wedding. Then
when you're married . . . It's crazy. You can have it whenever you want. You wake up. She's there. You come home
from work. She's there. So, all the sex-planning talk is over.
And the wedding-planning talk. We can sit up here and
bullshit the night away, but I can't have a five-minute conversation with Beth. But, I'm not putting the blame on her.
We've just got nothing to talk about.

The Verdict

Twentieth Century-Fox (A Zanuck/Brown Production), 1982
Screenplay by David Mamet
Based on a novel by Barry Reed
Directed by Sidney Lumet

Time: 1982
Place: Boston
Frank Galvin is a heavy-drinking, middle-aged lawyer spe-
cializing in criminal law and personal injury. Once successful, he realizes, after a string of failed cases, that he is
losing his grip. He's reduced to scanning the obituaries in
the newspapers and attending funerals, pretending to be
an acquaintance of the deceased. He passes out his business
card to the bereaved families, should they "need anything"
(his services).

Mickey Morrissey, an older lawyer and associate of Galvin's, is concerned about him and throws a medical mal-
practice case Galvin's way. Having procrastinated for months
and with the trial date approaching, Galvin is forced to

scramble to prepare himself to try the case of *Deborah Ann Kaye* v. *St. Catherine Laboure Hospital, et al.*

A young, healthy mother, Deborah Kaye, is admitted to St. Catherine's to deliver her third child. She is given the anesthetic and ends up in an irreversible coma, attached to machines in a nursing home. The woman's family, devout Catholics, must sue the doctors and hospital, which is run by the Archdiocese, because they cannot meet the expenses of "perpetual care" for Deborah.

Galvin, divorced and a disillusioned Catholic, is tempted to accept a substantial out-of-court settlement offered by the Archdiocese. He hears, however, from an informant/ doctor at the hospital, that, unquestionably, negligence on the part of the attending physicians was responsible for Deborah Kaye's coma. Galvin turns the settlement offer down and decides to pursue the case to trial and reveal the facts.

He is confronted by Ed Concannon, a well-heeled and ruthless attorney who is representing the hospital. Mickey refers to Concannon as "the Prince of Fuckin' Darkness." With relentless determination to reveal the truth, Galvin builds his case. This is his closing statement to the jury.

———

GALVIN
(in front of the full jury box)
You know, so much of the time we're lost. We say "Please, God, tell us what is right. Tell us what's true. There is no justice. The rich win, the poor are powerless . . ." We become tired of hearing people lie. After a time we become dead. A little dead. We start thinking of ourselves as victims.

(pause)
And we *become* victims.

(pause)

And we *become* weak . . . and *doubt* ourselves, and doubt our *institutions* . . . and doubt our *beliefs* . . . we say for example, "The law is a sham—there *is* no law . . . I was a fool for having *believed* that there was."

(*beat*)

But today *you* are the law. *You* are the law . . . And not some *book* and not the *lawyers,* or the marble *statues* and the trappings of the court . . . all that they are is *symbols*.

(*beat*)

Of our desire to be just . . .

(*beat*)

All that they are, in effect, is a *prayer* . . .

(*beat*)

A fervent, and a frightened prayer.

(*beat*)

In my religion we say, "Act as if you had faith, and faith will be given to you."

(*beat*)

If. If we would have faith in *justice,* we must only believe in *ourselves.*

(*beat*)

And *act* with justice.

(*beat*)

And I believe that there is justice in our hearts.

(*beat*)

Thank you.

The Big Chill

Carson Productions Group, Ltd./Columbia Delphi Production
(Produced by Michael Shamberg), 1983
Screenplay by Lawrence Kasdan and Barbara Benedek
Directed by Lawrence Kasdan

Time: 1982
Place: Southeast, U.S.A.
Nick, in his mid-thirties, a Vietnam vet and former radio talk-show host, arrives at the well-appointed home of his friends Harold and Sarah Cooper. He and other friends, who graduated about ten years ago from the University of Michigan, have gathered at Harold and Sarah's for the reception after the funeral of their friend Alex, who committed suicide while living in a smaller house on the Coopers' property.

The friends decide to stay for the weekend and have an impromptu bittersweet reunion.

Nick is adrift, with no permanent address. He's a low-level drug dealer and takes drugs himself. The day after the funeral reception Nick is tinkering with Harold's video camera. He does a mock interview of himself, playing both interviewer and subject.

NICK
(Interviewer)
So you came back from Vietnam a "changed man."
(Guest)
Well, why don't you just tell *everybody*.
(Interviewer)
And then in 1972 you returned to the University of Michigan to enter the doctoral program in psychology. But you just couldn't seem to finish that dissertation.

(Guest)

I *could* have. I *chose* not to. I'm not hung up on this completion thing.

(Interviewer)

Then it was on to a series of jobs, all of which you quit.

(Guest)

What are you getting at? I was evolving. I'm *still* evolving.

(Interviewer)

But your real fame came as a radio psychologist on KQID in San Francisco.

(Guest)

I wouldn't call it "fame." I had a small, deeply disturbed following. Are we almost done here?

(Interviewer)

What are you doing now—or I should say, what have you evolved into now?

(Guest)

Oh . . . I'm in sales.

(Interviewer)

What are you selling?

(Guest, mumbles)

I don't have to answer that.

(looks off camera, as if to lawyer)

Do I have to answer that?

(HAROLD sticks his head in the living room.)

[HAROLD

Nick, we're leaving now. Have you seen Chloe?]

NICK

(as Interviewer, perturbed)

Harold, we're on the air here.

(as Guest)

Hey, sorry, I gotta go.

(as Interviewer)

Just answer that last question!

(as Guest, grabs his own shirt, roughly)
Listen, pal, I *said* I've got to go!

Lianna

United Artists Classics/A Winwood Production
(Produced by Jeffrey Nelson and Maggie Renzi), 1983
Screenplay by John Sayles
Directed by John Sayles

Time: 1982
Place: New Jersey college town
In a small Northeastern college town, Lianna, thirtyish, a
loving mother of two, has recently left her boorish,
philandering husband (a film professor), and set up
housekeeping on her own.

While Lianna struggles with her new independence, living
apart from her children, she has a surprising revelation:
She finds herself attracted to her psychology teacher at
night school, a woman. Ruth, in her early forties, is similarly
drawn to her pupil.

Lianna and Ruth have their first dinner together, at Ruth's
house, and later in the evening, while relaxing on the couch,
Ruth asks Lianna if she remembers her first crush. At this
point, Ruth and Lianna have not discussed their mutual
attraction.

[RUTH
Right. Do you remember your first crush?]
LIANNA
My first crush . . . I used to go to camp up north in the

summer. There was this one counselor, she was fifteen,
maybe sixteen. I was so glad when I got her squad. She
taught us field hockey. I had a sort of crush on her. . . .
No. I was in love with her. . . . The girl I bunked with,
her name was Virginia Dobbs, she was skinny—about as
unattractive as I was—she discovered that this counselor
was sneaking out of the cabin late every night. So we started
following her. She'd meet this guy. He was a lifeguard from
the boy's camp, he came in a canoe. Virginia and I hid by
the boathouse and watched them on this little strip of beach.
We could see his bare bottom shining white in the moon-
light. I couldn't believe her breasts. We kept trying not to
giggle—not that we thought anything was funny, just that
nervous kind of giggling when you're scared and fascinated
at the same time. When we got back to the cabin, Virginia
and I would slip under the covers together in the bottom
bunk, my bunk, and we'd cuddle and whisper, and then
Virginia would show me how they did it, and it was like
playing at first, Virginia calling out the lifeguard's name. Then
we'd start to get excited and I'd pretend Virginia had breasts.
. . . I haven't thought about that in a really long time.

Silkwood

**Twentieth Century-Fox/ABC Motion Pictures
(Produced by Mike Nichols and Michael Hansman), 1983
Screenplay by Nora Ephron and Alice Arlen
Directed by Mike Nichols**

Time: 1970s
Place: Karen's home in Oklahoma
This film is based on the true story of Karen Silkwood, a
nuclear plant worker at the Kerr-McGee facility in Okla-

homa. When her car ran off the road under suspicious circumstances, some believed she was murdered because she had evidence that the Kerr-McGee plant was unsafe.

Karen is in her late twenties and separated from her common-law husband and young children. She lives with her lover, Drew, and her friend, Dolly.

At the Kerr-McGee plant, there are incidents of accidental contamination by radioactive materials through human or mechanical error. One day Karen is contaminated and must undergo the violent decontamination process. She is scrubbed raw under hot showers in an effort to rid her of the contaminant.

After the ordeal Karen goes home to Drew and Dolly. Traumatized and sore after the decontamination, Karen takes another shower. After the shower she walks outside and sits on the porch with Drew.

———

KAREN

My hair feels awful.
> (beat)

Wish I had some of that conditioner.
> (beat)

I'm going to call my mother, ask her to send some up.
> (beat)

She called me up a couple of days ago.
> (mimicking her mother's deep Texas accent)

"Karen, I been thinkin' 'bout yer nails. How are yer nails? You bitin' 'em or you takin' care of 'em?"
> (in her own voice)

"I'm taking good care of them, Mama."
> (her mother again)

"Don't you cut the cuticles now, y'hear."
> (She shakes her head.)

                        [DREW
I wish I could take care of you better.]
                        KAREN
                     (after a beat)
I remember in high school her saying, "Now what d'you
want to take that science class for? There's no girls in that
science class. You take Home Ec why don't you—that's the
way to meet the nice boys." "Mama," I said. "There ain't
no boys in Home Ec. The boys are in the science class."
She hated when I said "ain't."
                      (beat)
At least he doesn't talk when he doesn't have something to
say.
                        [DREW
Who?]
                        KAREN
My dad.

The Brother from Another Planet

Cinecom International Films (Produced by Peggy Rajski
and Maggie Renzi), 1984
Screenplay by John Sayles
Directed by John Sayles

Time: 1984
Place: Harlem
The Brother is a mute, black alien, indistinguishable from
human beings, who crash-lands on Ellis Island and ends
up wandering through Harlem. One of the people he encounters is Randy Sue. A friend of hers has found the Brother
and brought him to her. She has generously offered him a
place to stay for a while, in her modest but warm apartment.
    Randy Sue, a white woman in her early thirties, was

raised in Alabama and had a traditional Southern upbring-ing. While in her twenties she moved north to the East Coast and fell in love with Earl, a black man. Early in their relationship Earl left her, and she now lives in Harlem with their child, Earl, Jr., and her mother-in-law. While Earl, Jr., and the Brother watch TV, Randy Sue talks to the Brother.

––––––––

RANDY SUE

You don't talk, huh? Well that's good. You don't talk you don't talk people into things. You don't talk you don't lie. My Bobby, you know, he's off living with this other girl. He's always talkin' people into things. He's great at that. You know, if they had it in the Olympics he'd win a gold medal. Bobby. Bobby. I met him up this place, you know, and he comes up to me an' he starts talkin, next thing you know, I'm big as a house with Little Earl here. Bobby's sweet, you know, if he doesn't get bored with you or see somethin' he likes better right across the street.

(pause)

You eat pork?

(pause)

Well, you don't eat it, you're outa luck tonight 'cause that's what we're having. Course, you don't talk so you can't complain, right?

(pause)

The mother's gonna come home an' complain now. Like she's some kind of gourmet cook. My philosophy is you got complaints, you just go eat somewhere else. You know, my mama made us clean our plates, every night, and she couldn't cook worth shit. She couldn't cook—like—pudding, you know? She'd cook chocolate pudding, and there'd be these big lumps, these *tumors* in it. You know like what people with breast cancer have cut out. There were six of us. I'm

from Alabama, can you handle that? Pidcock, Alabama. I'm
up here takin' care of the old lady and Little Earl and he's
off makin' time with some girl doesn't have any more sense
than I did when I was her age. If they could see me now.
Where you from? You look like you might be from the
South—

(pause)

No way I'm goin back there, not with Little Earl I'm not.
I burned my bridges.

(pause)

Here, you look like you might be about Bobby's size. Serves
him right, he didn't even come by to pick up his stuff.

(pause)

You know this stuff is gonna rot your brain. Sometimes I
feel like I have been taken for a slave up here. You know,
they have 'em, white slaves. The Arabs keep them. It's like
a whole 'nother world up here, a whole 'nother planet. You
know, with all the talkin' he did, Bobby didn't ever tell
how I couldn't go back. Not unless I give up Little Earl,
and that's the one thing I'm not ever gonna do. You know,
that's the only thing Bobby gave me that he didn't take
back later. I got to stay and keep Little Earl safe from all
that mess outside. The shoes are almost new, he didn't
wear 'em but once or twice.

(pause)

The mother's okay, you know, she's got a good heart, but
she resents it because she thinks I drove Bobby away from
her. He said he couldn't *wait* to get out of here, he said it
was like being in jail here. And now he says that he's really
in love and all this stuff, like he doesn't remember that he
said the exact same things to me when we first met. Like
I got no memory, like I got no feelings.

(pause)

The worst is being alone here all day. Little Earl, yeah,

but he talks just about as much as you do, and when he does, he's five years old.

> · *(pause)*

Sometimes I just think I'm gonna go crazy livin' up here like this.

> *(pause)*

You eat pork?

The Breakfast Club

MCA/Universal, 1985
Produced by Ned Tanen and John Hughes
Written by John Hughes
Directed by John Hughes

Time: March 24, 1985
Place: Shermer High School, Shermer, Illinois
Five high-school students, Brian, Andy, Alison, Clair, and John, must spend Saturday in detention at the school library. Their assignment is to write a thousand-word essay describing who they are. They all come from different cliques in their school and are described by one of the group as being "a brain, an athlete, a basket case, a princess, and a criminal." Although they don't know each other as they start the detention, by the end of the day each has revealed something about himself and all five become friends.

Andy, "the athlete," explains why he got detention.

ANDY

Do you guys know what I did to get in here? I taped Larry Lester's buns together. Yeah, you know him? Well then, you know how hairy he is, right? Well, when they pulled the tape off, most of his hair came off and some skin too. And the bizarre thing is, is that I did it for my old man. I tortured this poor kid because I wanted him to think I was cool. He's always going off about, you know, when he was in school, all the wild things he used to do, and I got the feeling that he was disappointed that I never cut loose on anyone, right? So, I'm sitting in the locker room and I'm taping up my knee and Larry's undressing a couple lockers down from me and he's kinda, kinda skinny, weak, and I started thinking about my father and his attitude about weakness, and the next thing I knew I, I jumped on top of him and started wailing on him. Then my friends, they just laughed and cheered me on. And afterwards, when I was sittin' in Vernon's office, all I could think about was Larry's father and Larry having to go home and explain what happened to him. And the humiliation, the fucking humiliation he must have felt. It must have been unreal. I mean, how do you apologize for something like that? There's no way. It's all because of me and my old man. God, I fucking hate him. He's like, he's like this mindless machine I can't even relate to anymore. "*Andrew*, you've got to be number one. I won't tolerate any losers in this family. Your intensity is for shit." You son of a bitch. You know, sometimes I wish my knee would give and I wouldn't be able to wrestle anymore. He could forget all about me.

MONOLOGUE PROFILE REFERENCE CHART

Key

MOMAFSC	Museum of Modern Art Film Studies Center, New York City
LC	Theatre Collection, New York Public Library at Lincoln Center, New York City
NYU	Script Collection, Elmer Holmes Bobst Library, New York University, New York City

Film	Character	Character's Occupation	Age
M	Murderer	Murderer	30s
I Am a Fugitive from a Chain Gang	James Allen	Soldier Returned from War	20s
It Happened One Night	Shapeley	Traveling Salesman	40s
Mutiny on the Bounty	John Byam	Midshipman	20s
Mr. Deeds Goes to Town	Babe	Newspaper Reporter	20s
Things to Come	Roxana	None Indicated	20s
The Life of Emile Zola	Emile Zola	Writer	—
The Life of Emile Zola	Emile Zola	Writer	—
Drums Along the Mohawk	Gil Martin	Pioneer	20s
Mr. Smith Goes to Washington	Joseph Paine	U.S. Senator	50s
Mr. Smith Goes to Washington	Jefferson Smith	New U.S. Senator	20s
Knute Rockne, All American	Knute Rockne	Football Coach	40s
Grapes of Wrath	Tom Joad	Migrant Worker	20s
The Westerner	Cole Hardin	Cowboy	20s
The Lady Eve	Jean	Con Artist	20s

Time Period	Setting	Original Actor	Source of Monologue	Page No.
1931	German City	Peter Lorre	Published Screenplay	3
Post–World War I	East Coast	Paul Muni	Published Screenplay	5
1934	On a Bus	Roscoe Karns	Published Screenplay	7
1790s	England	Franchot Tone	LC	10
1930s	New York City	Jean Arthur	LC	13
The "Future" 1970s	Prison Cell	Margaretta Scott	Published Screenplay	15
1890s	Paris	Paul Muni	LC	17
1890s	Paris	Paul Muni	LC	20
Revolutionary War	Mohawk Valley, N.Y. State	Henry Fonda	Dartmouth College, I. Thalberg film collection	23
1930s	Washington, D.C.	Claude Rains	Published Screenplay	26
1930s	Washington, D.C.	James Stewart	Published Screenplay	28
1920s–1930s	Locker Room	Pat O'Brien	MGM/UA Script Archives	30
1930s	California	Henry Fonda	Published Screenplay	32
1843	Texas	Gary Cooper	LC	34
1941	On Board a Luxury Liner	Barbara Stanwyck	MOMAFSC	36

Film	Character	Character's Occupation	Age
Meet John Doe	Ann Mitchell	Newspaper Reporter	20s
Hail the Conquering Hero	Woodrow Truesmith	Mayor-Elect	Early 20s
It's a Wonderful Life	George Bailey	Savings & Loan President	20s
Treasure of the Sierra Madre	Howard	Prospector	60s
Adam's Rib	Amanda	Lawyer	Late 30s
Adam's Rib	Adam	Lawyer	40s
A Letter to Three Wives	Deborah Bishop	Housewife	20s
All the King's Men	Willie Stark	Politician	30s
The African Queen	Charlie Allnutt	Supply Boat Operator	40s
The Day the Earth Stood Still	Klaatu	Interplanetary Emissary	N.A.
East of Eden	Abra	None Indicated	20s
On the Waterfront	Father Barry	Priest	40s
On the Waterfront	Terry Malloy	Dock Worker	20s
La Strada	Gelsomina	Circus Performer's Assistant	Approx. 20

Time Period	Setting	Original Actor	Source of Monologue	Page No.
1941	Midwest City	Barbara Stanwyck	LC	38
1944	Oakridge, California	Eddie Bracken	LC	40
1930s	Bedford Falls, New England	James Stewart	MOMAFSC	42
1924	Mexico	Walter Huston	Published Screenplay	45
1949	New York City	Katharine Hepburn	Published Screenplay	46
1940	New York City	Spencer Tracy	Published Screenplay	48
Late 1940s	Suburban Town	Jeanne Crain	Private Collection	50
1920s and 1930s	American South	Broderick Crawford	Published Screenplay	52
1915	Central Africa	Humphrey Bogart	Published Screenplay	56
1951	Washington, D.C.	Michael Rennie	20th Century-Fox Script Archives	59
1917	Salinas Valley, California	Julie Harris	LC	61
1950s	Hoboken, New Jersey, Docks	Karl Malden	Published Screenplay	63
1950s	Taxicab	Marlon Brando	Published Screenplay	66
"An Earlier Time"	Italy	Guilietta Mesina	MOMAFSC	67

Film	Character	Character's Occupation	Age
Night of the Hunter	Harry Powell	Evangelist/ Preacher	30s
The Goddess	Emily Ann	High School Student	Teens
The Goddess	Emily Ann	High School Student	Teens
The Long, Hot Summer	Ben Quick	Jack-of-All- Trades	Early 20s
Hiroshima Mon Amour	The Woman	Actress	30
The Apartment	Fran Kubelik	Elevator Operator	20s
The Apartment	C. C. "Bud" Baxter	Junior Executive	30s
Elmer Gantry	Elmer Gantry	Traveling Salesman	30s
Elmer Gantry	Lulu Bains	Prostitute	30s
Breakfast at Tiffany's	O. J. Berman	Agent	Late 30s
Breakfast at Tiffany's	Holly Golightly	"Party Girl"	Early 20s
Jules and Jim	Catherine	Teacher/ Illustrator	Late 20s
Jules and Jim	Jim	Not Indicated	Late 20s
The Hustler	Eddie Felson	Professional Pool Player	Late 20s
The Hustler	Eddie Felson	Professional Pool Player	Late 20s

Time Period	Setting	Original Actor	Source of Monologue	Page No.
1930s	Midwest Town	Robert Mitchum	Published Screenplay	69
1940s	Small Town, U.S.A.	Kim Stanley	Published Screenplay	70
1940s	Small Town, U.S.A.	Kim Stanley	Published Screenplay	72
1958	Mississippi	Paul Newman	20th Century-Fox Script Archives	73
August 1957	Hiroshima	Emmanuelle Riva	Published Screenplay	75
1960	New York City	Shirley MacLaine	Published Screenplay	77
1960	New York City	Jack Lemmon	Published Screenplay	79
1920s	Midwest	Burt Lancaster	LC	80
1920s	Midwest	Shirley Jones	LC	82
1961	Manhattan	Martin Balsam	Private Collection	83
1961	Manhattan	Audrey Hepburn	Private Collection	84
1912–1920s	France	Jeanne Moreau	Published Screenplay	85
1912–1920s	France	Henri Serre	Published Screenplay	88
1961	City, U.S.A.	Paul Newman	Published Screenplay	89
1961	City, U.S.A.	Paul Newman	Published Screenplay	91

Film	Character	Character's Occupation	Age
To Kill a Mockingbird	Mayella Ewell	Farmgirl	Early 20s
To Kill a Mockingbird	Atticus Finch	Lawyer	Late 40s
Freud	Cecily	Schoolgirl	Early 20s
Freud	Mrs. Koertner	Cecily's Mother	40s
Dr. Strangelove	President Muffley	President of U.S.A.	40s
Inside Daisy Clover	Raymond Swan	Major Film Studio Executive	40s
The Pawnbroker	Sol Nazerman	Pawnbroker	45
Persona	Alma	Nurse	25
In the Heat of the Night	Delores Purdy	Schoolgirl	16
Easy Rider	George Hanson	Lawyer	20s
Last Summer	Rhoda	High School Student	Teens
Goodbye, Mr. Chips	Mr. Chipping	Latin Master at Boy's Academy	80
Five Easy Pieces	Bobby Dupea	Oil Rig Worker	20s

Time Period	Setting	Original Actor	Source of Monologue	Page No.
1932	Alabama	Collin Wilcox	LC	92
1932	Alabama	Gregory Peck	LC	93
1890s	Paris	Susannah York	LC	95
1890s	Paris	Eileen Herlie	LC	96
1960s	Washington, D.C.	Peter Sellers	MOMAFSC	97
1930s	Hollywood	Christopher Plummer	Warner Bros. Script Archives	100
1963	Spanish Harlem, New York City	Rod Steiger	LC	102
1966	Swedish Coast	Bibi Andersson	Published Screenplay	104
1967	Mississippi	Quentin Bell	LC	107
1969	On the Road	Jack Nicholson	Published Screenplay	108
1969	Affluent Summer Beach Colony	Cathy Burns	NYU	110
1940s	England	Peter O'Toole	LC	112
1970	Puget Sound	Jack Nicholson	Dialogue Taken from Screen	114

Film	Character	Character's Occupation	Age
Klute	Bree Daniels	Call Girl	Late 20s
Who Is Harry Keller-man . . .	Linda Kaiser	Aspiring Actress	34
Last Tango in Paris	Paul	Out-of-Work Journalist	40s
Paper Moon	Trixie Delight	Dancer	30s
The Way We Were	Katie Morosky	Radio Station Worker	20s
The Conversation	Harry Caul	Electronics Surveillance Professional	44
Scenes from a Marriage	Johan	Professor	40s
Harry and Tonto	Harry	Retired Teacher	70s
Dog Day Afternoon	Heidi	Wife and Mother	20s
Dog Day Afternoon	Sonny	None Indicated	Mid 30s
Next Stop, Greenwich Village	Larry Lapinsky	Struggling Actor	20s
Carrie	Margaret White	Carrie's Mother	Late 30s
All the President's Men	Carl Bernstein	Newspaper Reporter	20s

Time Period	Setting	Original Actor	Source of Monologue	Page No.
1971	New York City	Jane Fonda	LC	116
1971	New York City	Barbara Harris	LC	117
1972	Paris	Marlon Brando	Published Screenplay	120
1930s	Midwest	Madeline Kahn	Dialogue Taken from Screen	122
1930s–1960s	New York City	Barbra Streisand	Private Collection	124
1974	San Francisco	Gene Hackman	MOMAFSC	125
1970s	Sweden	Erland Josephson	Published Screenplay	128
1974	New York City	Art Carney	MOMAFSC	130
Aug. 22, 1972	Brooklyn	Susan Peretz	Warner Bros. Script Archives	131
Aug. 22, 1972	Brooklyn	Al Pacino	Warner Bros. Script Archives	133
1953	Greenwich Village, New York City	Lenny Baker	NYU	134
1976	Midwest Suburb	Piper Laurie	CG Prods., Inc.	136
June 1972	Washington, D.C.	Dustin Hoffman	Warner Bros. Script Archives	138

Film	Character	Character's Occupation	Age
Network	Howard Beale	Television Newscaster	50s
An Unmarried Woman	Erica	Housewife & Mother	Late 30s
An Unmarried Woman	Saul	Painter	Mid 40s
Annie Hall	Alvy Singer	Comedian & Writer	Late 30s
The Goodbye Girl	Eliot Garfield	Actor	30s
Autumn Sonata	Eva	Journalist/ Author	Late 30s
Interiors	Joey	Writer	20s
Kramer vs. Kramer	Ted	Advertising Executive	30s
Kramer vs. Kramer	Joanna	Housewife & Mother	30s
Norma Rae	Reuben	Union Organizer	30s
Norma Rae	Norma Rae	Textile Worker	32
Apocalypse Now	Kurtz	Army Captain	40s
Breaking Away	Mike	High School Student	17

Time Period	Setting	Original Actor	Source of Monologue	Page No.
1975	New York City	Peter Finch	MOMAFSC	139
1977	New York City	Jill Clayburgh	NYU	141
1977	New York City	Alan Bates	NYU	143
1977	New York City	Woody Allen	Published Screenplay	144
1977	New York City	Richard Dreyfuss	Dialogue Taken from Screen	146
1978	Southern Norway	Liv Ullmann	Published Screenplay	148
1978	Long Island Beach House	Marybeth Hurt	Published Screenplay	152
1979	New York City	Dustin Hoffman	NYU	154
1979	New York City	Meryl Streep	NYU	156
1979	Georgia	Ron Liebman	20th Century-Fox Script Archives	157
1979	Georgia	Sally Field	20th Century-Fox Script Archives	159
1970s	Cambodia	Marlon Brando	Dialogue Taken from Screen	161
1979	Indiana	Dennis Quaid	MOMAFSC	163

Film	Character	Character's Occupation	Age
The Great Santini	Colonel "Bull" Meecham	Air Corps Training Commander	40s
The Great Santini	Colonel "Bull" Meecham	Air Corps Training Commander	40s
Manhattan	Isaac Davis	TV Comedy Writer	Early 40s
Stardust Memories	Daisy	Concert Violinist	20s
Raging Bull	Joey La Motta	Prizefighter's Manager	30s
The French Lieutenant's Woman	Sarah Woodruff	Ladies' Companion/ Governess	Approx. 30
My Dinner with Andre	Wally	Actor	36
An Officer and a Gentleman	Sergeant Foley	Gunnery Sergeant	40s
Fanny and Alexander	Carl	Professor/ Scientist	40
Fanny and Alexander	Emilie	Actress	Late 20s
Fanny and Alexander	Aron	Works in Antique Shop	20
Poltergeist	Tangina	Clairvoyant	Ageless
Diner	Shrevie	Salesman	Early 20s
The Verdict	Frank Galvin	Lawyer	40s

Time Period	Setting	Original Actor	Source of Monologue	Page No.
1962	South Carolina	Robert Duvall	Warner Bros. Script Archives	164
1962	South Carolina	Robert Duvall	Warner Bros. Script Archives	165
1979	New York City	Woody Allen	Published Screenplay	167
1980	New Jersey Resort Hotel	Jessica Harper	Published Screenplay	169
1940s	New York City	Joe Pesci	MOMAFSC	171
1867	Lyme, England	Meryl Streep	Published Screenplay	172
1980s	New York City	Wallace Shawn	Published Screenplay	175
1982	Puget Sound	Louis Gossett, Jr.	MOMAFSC	180
1907	Uppsala, Sweden	Borje Ahlstedt	Published Screenplay	182
1907	Uppsala, Sweden	Ewa Froling	Published Screenplay	184
1907	Uppsala, Sweden	Mats Bergman	Published Screenplay	185
1981	California	Zelda Rubinstein	Dialogue Taken from Screen	187
1959	Baltimore	Daniel Stern	MGM/UA Archives	189
1982	Boston	Paul Newman	20th Century-Fox Script Archives	190

Film	Character	Character's Occupation	Age
The Big Chill	Nick	Drug Dealer	30s
Lianna	Lianna	Student	Late 20s
Silkwood	Karen Silkwood	Nuclear Plant Worker	Late 20s
The Brother from Another Planet	Randy Sue	Mother	20s
The Breakfast Club	Andy	High School Student	Teens

Time Period	Setting	Original Actor	Source of Monologue	Page No.
1980s	American Southeast	William Hurt	Private Collection	193
1982	New Jersey College Town	Linda Griffiths	Private Collection	195
1970s	Oklahoma	Meryl Streep	Private Collection	196
1984	Harlem, New York City	Caroline Aaron	Private Collection	198
1980s	Illinois	Emilio Estevez	Dialogue Taken from Screen	201

AFTERWORD

This section contains comments from theater and film professionals. It is intended to give the reader a broad and varied perspective on the monologue as an audition or study piece. We asked these professionals to mention some guidelines that they feel are important for an actor preparing an audition.

Deborah Brown, casting director
- Choose something close to yourself
- Do something appropriate to the *audition situation*. Ms. Brown related an experience where an actor was auditioning in a room where the heat had gone off. The actor proceeded to take off all his clothes as he did a monologue from *Richard III*. Not only did the striptease distract from his acting and was inappropriate to the piece, but the auditioners were worried about the mental health of the actor. He did not get the part.

  Another time Ms. Brown was auditioning actors for the role of a street hood in a movie. An actor came in and pointed a knife at Ms. Brown's neck! Don't carry realism too far!
- If the writers are present at the audition and you are reading something they have written, stick religiously to *their* lines. Trust their words, don't change them around. Remember even every "um" or "uh" has usually been written for a reason.
- Be businesslike. Try not to leave your belongings in the audition room and have to come back for them.
- Don't ask to do the audition over.
- Keep props and chatter to a minimum.

Griffin Dunne, actor/producer

- Don't do a show-off piece if you don't relate to it. Portray something that you're comfortable with.
- If you make a mistake in an audition, keep going and incorporate your mistakes into the piece. Dunne remembers, "When I did a monologue in the film *After Hours,* I couldn't stop in the middle if I made an error. When I did make a mistake, I tried to incorporate it into the monologue and keep an improvisational quality to the piece. The editor of the film can worry about putting the whole thing together."
- "When I auditioned for Uta Hagen's class doing Holden Caulfield's speech from *The Catcher in the Rye,* I was so nervous I forgot all my lines. But I knew basically what Holden was saying. I knew the through line of the speech, so I kept going and ended up in Uta's class."

Jane Feinberg, casting director

- If you're auditioning with a monologue in an office, choose something short and light.
- Don't overact at the audition. Try to give the essence of the character and not a complete performance.
- "Once I was reading actors for the part of a hijacker in a movie with John Travolta. I was reading Travolta's part. One young man came in, began reading his lines, suddenly grabbed me, knocking me to the floor, and proceeded to straddle me and inadvertently ripped my stockings. I was terrified and wouldn't suggest that any actor behave in such a way, but the guy got the part. It just goes to show—there are *no* rules!"

Jane Hoffman, actress/teacher

- Take your time with the monologue.
- Need to tell it.
- Take the stage with it.

- There must be an urgency to it. By that, I don't mean to rush.
- Learn to break the monologue down. Make it personal and specific.
- Treat it like a conversation with the audience.

Julie Hughes, casting director
- Sometimes it's smart to choose a monologue that is similar in tone to the particular play or film that you're auditioning for.
- Don't walk in and make excuses.
- Remember, casting directors hope that everyone is *wonderful* so that the director will have many different choices.

James Earl Jones, actor
- Mr. Jones writes, "Whether an actor memorizes the text or reads the speech from a book, it is better not to waste energy and concentration trying to create a sense of imaginary characters in space to whom you speak but to deliver the speech straight out or straight into the text. The point is to create a strong sense of what you are saying with the text and why you are saying it, focused internally and filled with all your concentration, energy, and feelings."

Emily Mann, director
- Ms. Mann hopes to see ". . . an actor sustain the emotional and intellectual *truth* of the speech. . . . I also hope to see an actor embrace a particular writer's language and know what to do with it."

Paul McCrane, actor
- The monologue can be the most advantageous work for an actor, in that you create the whole environment.
- Have a friend watch, direct, or critique you.

- When you are called upon to speak directly to an audience, "endow the audience with character." Ask yourself, "*Who* am I talking to?"
- Barnard Hughes has said acting is often like "stringing beads on a necklace. First you have to find all the beads, then string them in the right order."
- I tend to hate auditions, period. One part of me has a particular aversion to monologues. But what keeps me going is to have a sense of what works best for me and going into an audition *prepared*. That's the best you can do.
- *You* have the *time* when you prepare a monologue. Approach auditions as opportunities to perform. Recognize it's an audition, of course, but think, "I've had my own rehearsal process. . . . They have invited me to perform."
- Set it up as if in a production. The audition, then, becomes "*my work*"; those auditioning you are the audience. It's my performance and "that space belongs to me." In the end you may do a brilliant monologue and they may say, "He's too short for the part." That's a business thing. My job, my interest, is in this art form, in controlling the situation, investing myself into it. Go in and do it and respect the moment.
- The character I played in a recent Broadway production of *The Iceman Cometh*, Parritt, listens to Hickey's (played by Jason Robards) monumental monologue. I listen to the monologue and try to understand its impact. If you have faith in your own reality in the present moment, you find yourself reacting in a true way. Robards has said he understands the words first, what's happening, and *then* makes decisions. *Know it. Understand it.* Then, what comes out of that understanding will be authentic.

Brian McEleney, actor/teacher

- Give thought to the *physical* life of the character and the monologue. It's not just about words.

- In selecting a monologue choose something that has *movement* in it, where something happens or changes within the monologue. Don't do monologues that are *just* stories, unless, in the telling of the story, something happens to the character. If you are doing two monologues in an audition, *one* should be "movement-oriented."

- The basic thing to achieve is to talk and be natural, but that is not enough for an actor. Beyond this, the actor should be creative, innovative, and bold in his or her work.

- As an actor, look for a monologue that is surprising. For example, in a monologue you may seem to be going in one direction and then, surprisingly, go in another. That's interesting.

- Because monologues for auditions are totally up to the actor, you can take all the time you need to prepare, to rehearse, and then show yourself at your best. Without rehearsal and preparation you get something superficial and on one emotional note.

- The monologue can be delivered, in an audition, to whomever you imagine—your best friend, your worst enemy. It's your secret and you can talk to whomever you want.

- Finally, I hope actors can be as *brave* as they can be. Bravery is the thing. Be big, bold, inventive, but still personally generous. Give all of yourself in it. Be committed to acting it. Ask yourself: "What is this life about, that I'm exploring?" Give it as much life as you can and be generous—as if you are presenting *yourself* up there, not some foreign unknown character. Expose something deep and important.

Elizabeth McGovern, actress

- When you audition, pretend whoever is there is a friend.
- Create a reason, imagine a reason where it's *very important, absolutely vital,* to speak these words. You *have* to say these things.
- Be clear about who it is you are talking to, if the monologue is addressed to someone.

Wally Nicita, casting director

- Don't act too broadly at your audition. Try to have a conversation. .
- Since I cast films, keep in mind that I need a person to be like the role.
- Try to be flexible and do what you're asked when a director gives you a direction.

Jean Passanante, producer

- Choose material that is close to yourself in terms of age and experience. Choose monologues that have a beginning, a middle, and an end. Choose something that has content.
- Don't take a *long* pause before you begin.
- Don't do phony accents.
- Tell the auditioners what they are going to hear.
- Don't overproduce your audition, i.e., too many props, furniture, costumes.
- Don't wear too much perfume or after-shave.
- Don't shake hands too hard.
- Don't be overly solicitous of the auditioners.
- Don't do breast-beating, soul-searching pieces. Remember, your goal is to *entertain* the auditioners.
- If possible, try to acquaint yourself with the audition space beforehand. Don't do something out of proportion to the space.

Austin Pendleton, actor/director/teacher

- Mr. Pendleton prefers monologues that are not addressed to another person. He prefers the following forms of monologues:

"When the actor is alone and talking to himself. For example, Tennessee Williams's *Small Craft Warnings*, which is a series of monologues. A bunch of people in a bar on the coast of California sit and talk to themselves. They also talk to each other, but three-quarters of that play is monologues and it's beautiful, beautiful writing."

"When the actor talks to the audience and doesn't involve another character, e.g., Shakespeare, Williams, Wilder's *Skin of Our Teeth*."

"When the actor has a telephone conversation. There are classics, like *The Sterile Cuckoo* and *Two for the Seesaw*."

- I was always doing Shakespeare and other "speeches" that were delivered to other people. Even when they're tirades, they're to *other* people, to isolated, other individual characters. And I always had a terrible time with it, making mistakes all the time. And then when I began to teach, I became aware of the difference in the work— the actors who did the one kind of monologue and people who did the other kind of monologue, meant to be delivered to other people. There's something inevitably arbitrary about taking a speech and delivering it with a set of realities and removing the set of realities that create it. But, if an actor really *wants* to do or *has* to do a monologue that is delivered to another person, they should get a friend of theirs to sit there. And they should rehearse it with them and bring the friend in and have the person sit with their back to the audience so they can look at them. Or, if the auditioners won't allow that, just rehearse it completely with the other person so that all their choices and all their work evolve from having worked with the other person.

- Don't read through the play once and then do all your work on the piece itself. Do your homework on the context of the monologue. Be aware of what the monologue comes out of in the play. So many auditions flounder because the monologues are just not worked on enough. They don't understand what they're talking about, in the literal sense.

- Know who the other people are you are talking about in the monologue. If you're going to do a monologue, work as if you were working on a play. You have to work on the whole play, and, then, part of that work you do is on the monologue. So that you have the history of the character's life in the play, and, going into the monologue, you have it thoroughly worked on. Go deep and wide. Context is more than important; its indispensable. People leave it out. Actors should use the monologue as a way of investigating the play. Even learn some of the rest of the play. You're only young once; you should really try to make it count!

- Don't take off without having roared along the runway. Or do the broad jump without taking a running start. Work on the scene that leads into the monologue. Play it. A monologue should be thought of as a scene, even when the person is all alone. Go and look up the screenplay. That's very important. Study it.

David Rotenberg, director

- Do something you *really* like that shows the auditioner who *you* are. Choose a monologue that allows *you* to shine through. Don't let the monologue upstage the actor.

- Don't *ever* apologize for your audition.

- Don't do something that shows a tremendous variety of emotions. Keep it simple.

- Don't do a "private moment." Don't take forever to prepare yourself to give the monologue.
- Don't dress funny.
- Be pleasant, low-key. Remember, the director is also thinking, "Do I want to have coffee with that person in the morning?"

Amy Saltz, director
- Pick material that you are comfortable with and that you think is a part you might realistically be cast in.
- Be prepared for the audition: *Know your lines.* Have a number of contrasting selections available, i.e., classical, contemporary, comic, serious.
- Be willing and able to make any changes in the monologue that the auditioner asks for.
- Don't upstage yourself.
- Don't be reticent about engaging in conversation with the director.
- Don't argue with the director. Express your point of view but don't make it imperative to prove your point.
- Question: When you ask for a monologue, what is it you hope for? Ms. Saltz's reply: "I look for any number of things—degree of personalization, depth, imagination, ability to handle language (if classic). Often it's just to get an idea of range and how the actor works. I feel the audition process is almost barbaric. Inadequate as it may be, it is the only system we have, so we must all learn to live with it. Don't try to second-guess or outsmart whoever you're auditioning for—you never really know what they are looking for. Set challenges for yourself so that the success or failure of the audition isn't dependent on whether or not you get the role. You can do a fabulous audition and not get the role for reasons that have nothing to do with you."

Paul Sorvino, actor

- Don't do something outside your age or experience, and don't do a dialect unless you know it cold.
- Don't go to the auditions hating the people that you are auditioning for. Go to auditions with the idea of sharing and giving something to the auditioners.
- Marlon Brando's rendition of the "Cry havoc" speech in the movie version of *Julius Caesar* inspired Mr. Sorvino to try the same speech at an audition for the Broadway show *Viva, Vivat Regina*. When he prepared the speech at home, his children were sleeping and he had to speak softly. At the audition Mr. Sorvino was, in his own words, "like a tiger jumping out of a cage." He performed at *too* high a level, and, needless to say, did not get the part. The moral: Prepare at home as if you were in an audition situation.

John Stix, director

- Choose something you feel you can do better than anyone else, something that inspires *you*.
- Do not overprepare. That is, don't "set" everything. Structure the piece but leave room for fresh thought and spontaneous behavior.
- Don't start too soon. Be in touch with the elements that feed you. But do not *indulge* yourself in endless waiting.
- When auditioning an actor for a specific role, I hope to see if the shoe fits. If for study, I hope to get some sense of their approach to work and, primarily, to get some measure of their imagination.

Daniel Swee, casting director

- I think there's a big difference between audition and class work. In class work the point is going to be to pick something that's going to help you grow the best and hone your craft as an actor. Whereas for an audition situation, if you're using the monologue as a general piece rather than using it to audition for a specific play, you should pick something that suits you. So much of that is simply being someone who has a good judgment of himself. I think one of the biggest problems is that people don't necessarily realize their type and general range and do not always pick material that is best suited for them. It doesn't show their strengths in a way that is going to direct them into the jobs that they're more likely to get.

- In general auditions I ask people to bring in two contrasting monologues—it may mean a classical and a contemporary, it may mean two contemporaries but of different sorts—people get the opportunity to show more than one side.

- Find a monologue that has "range" within it—that can be useful. Balance out the monologue in context and how much you want to take it out of context for the sake of dramatic purposes, so you can show yourself off and not, ultimately, serve the play. But you have to find the correct balance.

- Be prepared to work with the people auditioning you. Be prepared to listen to them and be able to try things they might suggest if they ask you to do it again.

- I'm looking for different things in different situations. If it's a general audition, I'm looking for as much of an idea of that person's talents and qualities as possible in that six-minute period. And the fact is, you *can* get something from someone in that short amount of time. Which is not to say you can completely rely on those things. But it's a way of getting to know someone who you have not had the opportunity yet to see in performance or other audition situations. And, someone who is trying to get you to know their work so you will bring them in for other auditions.

- The audition is an artificial process. Everyone's trying

to be artificially friendly. My feeling is, be as friendly as you can without being artificial about it. I don't want to go through life being surly; it takes a lot more energy to be surly and rude than to be friendly.

- Auditioners throw actors adjustments to see what they can do. Actors should be prepared for this.
- Know, in an audition, when it's good to sit down and become chatty—and when it's not.
- Don't bring a portfolio of pictures of yourself in past roles unless it's been requested.

Juliet Taylor, casting director

- Generally, in auditions for films, the actor is asked to read from the script or do a scene from the particular script, but, once, an actress auditioned by doing a very traumatic monologue and ended up throwing herself down on the floor in a puddle of tears. She was a bit much.
- When they call for a monologue, why not do a humorous monologue? In auditions, when you're *funny*, you're *funny*, and that's very rare. Comedy out of context can *still* be funny and can allow the auditioner to *see you*.

Peter Weller, actor

- No monologue is really a monologue if there is someone else in the room. It's a dialogue. But if it's only you in the room, there are two reasons why you would speak. One is to yourself. The other is to the camera, as if the camera were someone else. If it's an actor speaking to an audience, find someone in the audience, as if the audience were one person.
- It's the most difficult thing to execute. You must find an incredibly strong, visceral motive why anyone would speak as long as that.

Elizabeth Wilson, actress

- Always pick a strong object, or someone to speak the monologue to (*never* the audience or the person auditioning you, by the way).
- Don't do monologues you've written yourself. People hate that.
- Try to do monologues that are not terribly well known.

Michael Howard, teacher

- Actors *do* need to work on monologues, not only because they audition—the monologue is a mechanism to view an actor (not the best and not the only)—but also because the fact is there are many moments alone "on stage," in plays or in film. Whether there is a moment alone, or a moment when someone goes on at length with another person present, that moment has to be created within the context. So, an actor has to learn how to do that.
- As far as I'm concerned, an audition is a matter of *selling*. It is not a matter of *acting*. Acting is used, of course, but it is an arbitrary and mechanical moment where you are asked to take a certain gift, perhaps, a certain technical knowledge you have, and become a salesman.
- The monologue is an acting *"problem."* One needs to *practice* those moments, if you are lucky enough to get them in theater or in film. So, you need to practice with good material, not only to have choices to show yourself off in an audition, but to practice these "problems" that come up. This is one of the values of having a book of movie monologues.

SOURCES

M, 1931. Published Screenplay. Published by Lorrimar Publishers, London, England 1968.

I Am a Fugitive from a Chain Gang, 1932. Published screenplay, University of Wisconsin Press, 1981.

It Happened One Night, 1934. Published screenplay. In *Twenty Best Film Plays, Vol. I*, edited by John Gassner and Dudley Nichols, Crown Publishers, 1943.

Mutiny on the Bounty, 1935. Dialogue cutting continuity script, 1935. The Billy Rose Theatre Collection, New York Public Library at Lincoln Center, New York.

Mr. Deeds Goes to Town, 1936. Revised script. The Billy Rose Theatre Collection, New York Public Library at Lincoln Center, New York.

Things to Come, 1936. Published screenplay, Macmillan & Co., 1935.

The Life of Emile Zola, 1937. Published screenplay. In *Twenty Best Film Plays, Vol. I*, edited by John Gassner and Dudley Nichols, Crown Publishers, 1943.

Drums Along the Mohawk, 1939. Final script, 1939. Irving Thalberg Memorial Film Script Collection, Dartmouth College Library, Hanover, New Hampshire.

Mr. Smith Goes to Washington, 1939. Published screenplay. In *Twenty Best Film Plays, Vol. I*, edited by John Gassner and Dudley Nichols, Crown Publishers, 1943.

Knute Rockne, All American, 1940. Screenplay. Metro-Goldwyn-Mayer/United Artists Script Archives.

The Grapes of Wrath, 1940. Published screenplay. In *Twenty Best Film Plays, Vol. I*, edited by John Gassner and Dudley Nichols, Crown Publishers, 1943.

The Westerner, 1940. Shooting script. The Billy Rose Theatre Collection, New York Public Library at Lincoln Center, New York.

The Lady Eve, 1941. Shooting script. Museum of Modern Art Film Study Center, New York.

Meet John Doe, 1941. Shooting script. The Billy Rose Theatre Collection, New York Public Library at Lincoln Center, New York.

Hail the Conquering Hero, 1944. Release dialogue script, May 12, 1944. The Billy Rose Theatre Collection, New York Public Library at Lincoln Center, New York.

It's a Wonderful Life, 1946. Final shooting script, March 18, 1946, including added dialogue and scenes rewritten during production. Private collection.

The Treasure of the Sierra Madre, 1948. Published screenplay, University of Wisconsin Press, 1979.

Adam's Rib, 1949. Published screenplay. Published by Viking Press, 1972.

A Letter to Three Wives, 1949. Final script, May 19, 1948. Private collection.

All the King's Men, 1949. Published screenplay. In *Twenty Best Film Plays, Vol. I,* edited by John Gassner and Dudley Nichols, Crown Publishers, 1943.

The African Queen, 1951. Published screenplay. In *Agee on Film, Vol. II,* Grosset & Dunlap, 1967.

The Day the Earth Stood Still, 1951. Revised final draft, February 21, 1951. Twentieth Century-Fox Script Archives.

East of Eden, 1954. Final script, May 18, 1954. The Billy Rose Theatre Collection, New York Public Library at Lincoln Center, New York.

On the Waterfront, 1954. Published screenplay, Southern Illinois University Press, 1983.

La Strada, 1954. English translation of the screenplay. Museum of Modern Art Library, New York.

Hiroshima Mon Amour, 1959. Published screenplay, Grove Press, 1961.

The Night of the Hunter, 1955. Published screenplay. In *Agee on Film, Vol. II,* Grosset & Dunlap, 1967.

The Goddess, 1958. Published screenplay, Simon & Schuster, 1958.

The Long, Hot Summer, 1958. Final script, August 26, 1967. Twentieth Century-Fox Script Archives.

The Apartment, 1960. Published screenplay. In *The Apartment and The Fortune Cookie: Two Screenplays,* Praeger Film Library, Praeger Publishers, Inc., 1971.

Elmer Gantry, 1960. Dialogue continuity script, June 15, 1960. The Billy Rose Theatre Collection, New York Public Library at Lincoln Center, New York.

Breakfast at Tiffany's, 1961. Second-draft screenplay, June 22, 1960. Private collection.

Jules and Jim, 1961. Published screenplay, Simon & Schuster, 1968.

The Hustler, 1961. Published screenplay. In *Three Screenplays by Robert Rossen,* Anchor Books, Doubleday & Co., 1972.

To Kill a Mockingbird, 1962. First-draft screenplay. The Billy Rose Theatre Collection, New York Public Library at Lincoln Center, New York.

Freud, 1963. Final shooting script, February 10, 1962. The Billy Rose Theatre Collection, New York Public Library at Lincoln Center, New York.

Dr. Strangelove: Or, How I Learned to Stop Worrying and Love the Bomb, 1963. Dialogue script, January 1964. Museum of Modern Art Film Study Center, New York.

Inside Daisy Clover, 1965. Final script, January 28, 1965. Warner Brothers Script Archives.

The Pawnbroker, 1965. Revised script, August 28, 1963. The Billy Rose Theatre Collection, New York Public Library at Lincoln Center, New York.

Persona, 1966. Published screenplay. In *Persona and Shame: The Screenplays*, translated by Keith Bradfield, Grossman, 1972.

In the Heat of the Night, 1967. Release dialogue script, June 1967. The Billy Rose Theatre Collection, New York Public Library at Lincoln Center, New York.

Easy Rider, 1969. Published screenplay, Signet Books, New American Library, 1969.

Last Summer, 1969. Screenplay. Script Collection, Elmer Holmes Bobst Library, New York University.

Goodbye, Mr. Chips, 1969. Revised shooting script, February 6, 1968. The Billy Rose Theatre Collection, New York Public Library at Lincoln Center, New York.

Five Easy Pieces, 1970. Dialogue taken from the screen.

Klute, 1971. Screenplay, June 26, 1970. The Billy Rose Theatre Collection, New York Public Library at Lincoln Center, New York.

Who Is Harry Kellerman and Why Is He Saying Those Terrible Things About Me?, 1971. Continuity script. Courtesy of CBS Productions.

Last Tango in Paris, 1972. Published screenplay. Published by the Delacorte Press, 1973.

Paper Moon, 1973. Dialogue taken from the screen.

The Way We Were, 1973. Dialogue taken from the screen.

The Conversation, 1974. Screenplay, revised "draft in progress," November 13, 1972. Museum of Modern Art Film Study Center, New York.

Scenes from a Marriage, 1974. Published screenplay. In *The Marriage Scenarios*, English translation by Alan Blair, Pantheon Books, 1978.

Harry and Tonto, 1974. Final-draft screenplay, August 6, 1973. Museum of Modern Art Film Study Center, New York.

Dog Day Afternoon, 1975. Dialogue transcript plus revisions, August 8, 1975. Museum of Modern Art Film Study Center, New York.

Next Stop, Greenwich Village, 1975. Final-draft screenplay, March 10, 1975. Script Collection, Elmer Holmes Bobst Library, New York University.

Carrie, 1976. Final script, C. G. Productions, Inc.

All the President's Men, 1976. Final script, July 11, 1975. Warner Brothers Script Archives.

Network, 1976. Screenplay. Museum of Modern Art Film Study Center, New York.

An Unmarried Woman, 1977. Final-draft screenplay, November 1976. Script Collection, Elmer Holmes Bobst Library, New York University.

Annie Hall, 1977. Published screenplay. In *Four Films of Woody Allen,* Random House, 1982.

The Goodbye Girl, 1977. Dialogue taken from the screen.

Autumn Sonata, 1978. Published screenplay. In *The Marriage Scenarios,* English translation by Alan Blair, Pantheon Books, 1978.

Interiors, 1978. Published screenplay. In *Four Screenplays by Woody Allen,* Random House, 1982.

Kramer vs. Kramer, 1979. Screenplay, February 27, 1978. Script Collection, Elmer Holmes Bobst Library, New York University.

Norma Rae, 1979. Revised screenplay, March 13, 1978. Twentieth Century-Fox Script Archives.

Apocalypse Now, 1979. Dialogue taken from the screen.

Breaking Away, 1979. Screenplay, June 9, 1978. Museum of Modern Art Film Study Center, New York.

The Great Santini, 1979. Revised final-draft screenplay, June 28, 1978. Warner Brothers Script Archives.

Manhattan, 1979. Published screenplay. In *Four Screenplays by Woody Allen,* Random House, 1982.

Stardust Memories, 1980. Published screenplay. In *Four Screenplays by Woody Allen,* Random House, 1982.

Raging Bull, 1980. Revised screenplay, February 1, 1979. Museum of Modern Art Film Study Center, New York.

The French Lieutenant's Woman, 1981. Published screenplay, Little, Brown and Company, 1981.

My Dinner with Andre, 1981. Published screenplay, Grove Press, Inc., 1981.

An Officer and a Gentleman, 1982. Second-draft screenplay, February 21, 1979. Museum of Modern Art Film Study Center, New York.

Fanny and Alexander, 1982. Published screenplay. Translated from the Swedish by Alan Blair, Pantheon Books, 1982.

Poltergeist, 1982. Dialogue taken from the screen.

Diner, 1982. Final-draft screenplay, January 21, 1981. Metro-Goldwyn-Mayer/United Artists Script Archives.

The Verdict, 1982. Final-draft screenplay, November 23, 1981. Twentieth Century-Fox Script Archives.

The Big Chill, 1983. First-draft screenplay, July 16, 1982. Private collection.

Lianna, 1983. Dialogue continuity script. Private collection.

Silkwood, 1983. Shooting script, July 8, 1982. Private collection.

The Brother from Another Planet, 1984. Dialogue continuity script. Private collection.

The Breakfast Club, 1985. Second-draft screenplay, February 7, 1984. The Billy Rose Theatre Collection, New York Public Library at Lincoln Center, New York.

INDEX